Seeing Through the

*Living and Loving Better with Time Perspective Therapy:
Healing from the Past, Embracing the Present, Creating an Ideal Future*
by Philip G. Zimbardo and Rosemary K.M. Sword (Exposit, 2017)

Seeing Through the Grief

*A Time Perspective
Therapy Approach*

ROSEMARY K.M. SWORD *and*
PHILIP G. ZIMBARDO

Jefferson, North Carolina

ISBN (print) 978-1-4766-9414-6
ISBN (ebook) 978-1-4766-5182-8

LIBRARY OF CONGRESS AND BRITISH LIBRARY
CATALOGUING DATA ARE AVAILABLE

Library of Congress Control Number 2024009649

Front cover image: © Williu/Pixabay

Printed in the United States of America

Toplight is an imprint of McFarland & Company, Inc., Publishers

Box 611, Jefferson, North Carolina 28640
www.toplightbooks.com

Table of Contents

Acknowledgments   vii

Introduction   1

One. Grief, Loss, and Time Perspective Therapy   7
The Difference Between Grief, Mourning, and Loss 8 • The Difference
Between Loneliness and Being Alone 10 • But What Is Grief? 10 •
What Is "Normal" or "Common" Grief? 11 • How Long Will I
Mourn? 12 • Many Kinds of Grief 12 • Is Depression a Part of
Grief? 15 • Is Anxiety a Part of Grief? 17 • Is Stress a Part of
Grief? 19 • Religions and Spiritual Practices: How We Mourn—
Part 1 20 • The Elephant in the Room 22 • The Unkindest Things
to Say to a Mourner 23 • What If I Need Help? 27 • Take This
Quiz 28 • Zimbardo Time Perspective Inventory (ZTPI) Short
Form 29 • Five Main Time Perspectives in Time Perspective
Therapy 31 • A Balanced Time Perspective Leads to Greater
Stability 31 • Positive Effects 32 • To Sum Up 33

Two. The Past   37
The Genesis of Dying and Grief Research 38 • Rick and Rose: How
We Found Out Rick Was Dying 39 • Kübler-Ross's Five Stages of
Grief 40 • New Research 42 • Bias Toward the Past 43 •
Religions and Spiritual Practices: How We Mourn—Part 2 44 •
Similarities Between Grief and Post-traumatic Stress 46 • Changing
Past Negatives into Past Positives 51 • Noelle 52 • Noelle's Journey
from Past Negative to Past Positive 56 • Let's Get Started 58 •
Building Your Treasure Chest of Past Positive Memories 58 • Take
a Breath 59 • Good Memories 60 • A Good Night's Sleep 61 •
To Sum Up 66

Three. The Present   71
Caregivers 72 • Caregiver Stress 73 • Rick and Rose: Circle
of Support 74 • Help for Caregiver Stress 76 • Hospice
Care 78 • Rick and Rose: Everything Everywhere All at Once 79 •
The Vultures in the Room 81 • Crash Course in Narcissistic Personality

Symptoms 82 • Religions and Spiritual Practices: How We Mourn—
Part 3 83 • Parents, Children, Narcissists 85 • The Importance
of Wills 87 • Rick and Rose: The End of Physicality 88 • Bias
Toward the Present 90 • Temporary Present Fatalism 91 •
Noelle's Journey from Present Fatalism to Present Hedonism 94 •
Let's Get Started 95 • Be Kind to Yourself 96 • Be Here
Now 99 • Reconnect 100 • Flip the Switch and Then Go
Random 101 • To Sum Up 102

Four. **The Future**   107
The Importance of Nature 108 • Music and Grief 110 • Rose:
Facing the Future 112 • When Life Feels Out of Control 115 •
Religions and Spiritual Practices: How We Mourn—Part 4 117 •
Making Things Right 121 • Ho'oponopono 122 • Bias Toward
the Future 124 • Noelle's Journey into Her Brighter Future 126 •
Let's Get Started 128 • Our Brighter—and Different—Future 129 •
Setting Goals 131 • Looking Forward 132 • A Good Night's Sleep
Revisited 134 • Living a Life of Happiness and Meaning 136 •
To Sum Up 141

Epilogue   149

Glossary   153

Appendix I. ZTPI Questionnaire (Long Form)   155

Appendix II. Core Values   163

Appendix III. Character Strengths   167

Resources   171

Index   173

Acknowledgments

We would like to mention a legion of important but unsung people integral to book writing. You may have heard of "book" or "manuscript readers" and know them to be professionals who work for publishing houses. These folks are paid to read—what we imagine to be—mountains of manuscripts and determine whether they are worthy of consideration to be published. To us, this sounds like a cool job that wields a lot of power! So, logically, in large part we have them to bless for the books that grace our shelves, or that beam up at us from our tablets, or to which we listen while we're driving—and perhaps to shake a fist at and curse for our unpublished manuscripts.

There is another type of manuscript reader: those faithful people selected by the writer(s) to read what they have written and give honest feedback. Depending on the situation, these readers may receive sections or chapters of what is written, as it is written. At other times, readers may receive the entire manuscript when it is completed. A good mix of readers would include people familiar with the topic (in our case, it is grief) and/or method (which is time perspective therapy), as well as those who aren't familiar with the method. All should be familiar with the topic of grief, meaning that they should have lost a loved one. Those familiar with both topic and method can point out whether and where the writer has gone astray or if more information is needed. Those unfamiliar with the method can report to the writer whether there is confusion or unclear language, along with how to improve the presentation.

If a book is geared toward professionals or is a textbook, it is wise for the readers to have some knowledge of the topic or be in the field represented in the book. But if a book is intended for the general public, as this book is, then readers can (and, we dare say, *should*) come from different backgrounds. Moreover, these readers should be of varying ages. They can give vital feedback to the authors, who may then tweak, add, or completely rewrite sections of a manuscript based on what the readers recommend.

This brings us to the eight people whom we'll call "*our* readers." On occasion, some of these intrepid folks were what we'll call "focus group participants"; at other times, they sparked ideas for portions of this book. Our readers ranged in age from twenty-six to seventy-one. All had experienced the loss of a loved one. Four were familiar with time perspective therapy; the other four had heard it mentioned, but that is all. Our readers work in a wide range of fields, from space technology and data analysis to small business ownership and ocean research. They are, in alphabetical order, Nicki C., Ben Foley, Sarah Holter, Dee Ann Ventura, Scott Ventura, Ian Yannell, Liz Yannell, and Michael Yannell. Readers—we are eternally grateful for your invaluable input, insight, and honesty, as well as for your precious time. Really, we can't thank you enough!

Once again, we extend *mahalo nui loa* to Stanley Krippner, friend, colleague, and all-around good buddy, for his encouragement and support of time perspective therapy and our related endeavors. (As an aside, Stan was our late colleague and partner Rick Sword's psychology professor at Saybrook University.) Most recently, Stan, in his wonderful way of sharing, introduced us to the next three people we'd like to thank.

A heartfelt *dyakuyu* goes to psychotherapists Daria (Dasha) Buchinska, Natalia Khandobina and Olha Tereshchenko, and leaders of Edges, a Ukrainian non-profit. These dynamos, along with their team, assist their fellow Ukrainians with their expertise in mental health. During a recent *Zoom* meeting, as we discussed ways we can help them with time perspective therapy, we mentioned that we were writing this book. Natalia grew excited and shared that the people of Ukraine—citizens of all ages, including soldiers, veterans, and those who have suffered at the hands of Russian invaders, as well as hospitals and other institutions—need to learn how to cope with intense grief. They have suffered a tremendous loss of lives, homes, livelihoods, and communities. After this conversation, we were spurred on to complete this book quickly and include information and ways for people to cope—not just in our country but globally.

Finally, we'd like to extend our profound gratitude to our freelance editor and dear friend, Andria Coutoumanos. As an editor, Andie checked for all the things your English teacher would, like grammar and punctuation. But much more than that, she made us realize that the map we had in our minds, which we were following when writing this book, had been folded. When she pointed this out and helped us unfold the map, we were able to travel into territory in which, at first, we were reluctant to venture. The sparks that Andie and our readers produced lit our way on this journey and caused us to go deeper and travel farther than we originally thought we could, to places we didn't know existed. *Mahalo nui loa*, Andie.

Introduction

For the past several years, we, the authors, have been intent on writing a book about grief and loss. But the road to writing it took us on several detours.

We knew that time perspective therapy (TPT), the treatment we created in 2008–2009 along with colleague and partner Rick Sword to help people post-trauma, was also an efficacious therapy for depression, anxiety and stress—all of which can be experienced when one suffers a great loss or is in the process of grieving. Results of our TPT work were published in *The Time Cure* (2012). Then, a few months later, in 2013, the unimaginable happened: Rick was diagnosed with stage 3 gastric cancer. After a heroic effort to stave off the disease, Rick succumbed in June 2014. Over time, Rose used TPT to help herself process the ineffable loss of Rick, who was her husband, coparent, colleague/coworker, and constant companion. Not yet ready to write about grief, we—Phil and Rose—soldiered on and wrote *Living and Loving Better* (2017). It took a couple of years before we were both ready to commence serious discussions about researching and writing a grief and loss book.

During the early days of writing, as we outlined, researched and reviewed our comprehensive notes on grief, we were contacted by Michele Neff Hernandez and Michelle Dippel, both young widows and founding members of Soaring Spirits, an international organization. Their mission: to help all those who have lost a partner. We were elated to hear that years earlier, Michele and Michelle had read our book, *The Time Cure*, and integrated TPT into their grief program. But we were immensely gratified when they told us they had helped over three million people worldwide!

Spurred on by this good news, and certain that we were on to something valuable, we were now ready to dive into writing that much-needed book. Then we were contacted by Happify (*happify.com*), a popular tech-based self-help community. We had worked with Happify previously and developed a program to help people overcome post-traumatic stress.

This time, using TPT, we created a four-week track to help users cope with grief and loss.

While we were delighted we could help people through the Happify app, our grief book remained on the back burner. Phil grew busy with international work—bringing psychology to mental health professionals in China while continuing to educate people throughout Europe about time perspectives and his nonprofit, the Heroic Imagination Project. Meanwhile, Rose was occupied in working with Forum Media Polska (FMP), a Polish company that provides education, training and other services for those in the medical/mental health professions. (As an aside, more recently, Rose and Phil also worked with FMP on time perspective therapy, offering a course to Polish mental health professionals to help Ukrainians—soldiers, first responders and civilians displaced by the war in their country. Now Rose and Phil are working directly with Ukrainian psychologists to develop trauma and post-trauma protocols for veterans, the military, and civilians.)

During this time, our nation and the world began experiencing three things that exponentially increased the number of untimely deaths: (1) the COVID-19 pandemic, which raged on for years, to date killing seven million people worldwide; (2) the alarming number of gun-related deaths in the out-of-control mass shooting environment we live in here in the United States, where there are mass shootings at least once a day; and (3) the ever-increasing catastrophic climate change events wreaking extreme, unpredictable havoc everywhere.

In addition, both Phil and Rose have had brushes with mortality in the past year. We knew it was time to put the grief book back on the front burner, share what we've learned and teach our children how to grieve for us when the time comes! So …

What you are now reading is the fruit of our labors, *Seeing Through the Grief: A Time Perspective Therapy Approach*. In this book you'll learn the basics of our therapy and how it can help when people have suffered great loss and are grieving. These pages also include information about how people grieve around the world, what not to say to those in mourning, real-life experiences of grief and loss, and many more topics, some of which heretofore may have been considered forbidden.

Briefly, time perspective therapy is about checking our personal time perspective—that is, whether we view each time zone (past, present, and future) positively or negatively; if it's negative, then, by applying a dose of positive, we can gain a more balanced time perspective and therefore attain overall balance in our lives once again.

This simple method works when we get stuck in the past or in the present, especially when we are stuck in a negative experience. In time perspective therapy, these past recollections are considered *past negatives*. We might not realize that every day, *past negative* memories can cast a shadow over the way we think, see, and feel right now, in the present, as well as how we view the future. Time perspective therapy is helpful if we're stuck in a present behavior that we know is unhealthy, like *present fatalism*. A *past negative* experience can cause us to be *present fatalistic* and make us behave in ways we normally wouldn't or make us depressed when we're supposed to be happy.

Grief and loss can overshadow what has happened in the past. They can make things that are happening now seem overwhelming, and when this occurs, we can lose track of time and those people to whom we were once close or those things that used to bring us happiness. *Seeing Through the Grief* is a guidebook to help you move on in order to live a productive, joyful life. How? By refocusing on *past positives* instead of *past negatives*, becoming *selectively present hedonist*, and creating and working toward your different but brighter *future*.

Seeing Through the Grief is divided into four easy-to-follow sections:

"Chapter One: Grief, Loss, and Time Perspective Therapy"—You'll learn about the different kinds of grief and loss, the basics of our therapy and how it can assist *you*. A quiz is provided that helps determine which time perspectives—past positive/negative, present fatalism/hedonism, and future—you might need to improve in order to reclaim a more balanced life.

"Chapter Two: The Past"—Throughout our lives, and more often than not, it's helpful to remember the good times instead of difficult, challenging times. In this chapter, you'll discover the genesis of grief research as well as how different religions and spiritual practices approach death and grief. You'll also learn to remember and cherish past positive memories and how to recall them when you need them. This process is especially important if you've suffered trauma due to your personal loss.

"Chapter Three: The Present"—Sometimes when we are grieving, we are so deep in our despair that we forget how to experience even a little happiness here and now. In this chapter, we'll explore the present and help you rediscover how to insert some joy into your day-to-day, more gratifying life.

"Chapter Four: The Future"—Although facing the future may sometimes appear to be difficult and different from what we thought it would be, it's essential that we not lose sight of what is coming our way. In this chapter, you'll learn to make plans for your future and how to work toward making those plans your new reality, which will set you on the path to living a fuller and more meaningful life.

Seeing Through the Grief provides you with a set of simple tools that will help you see the big picture of your life. It will help you remember and cherish the good things in the past, appreciate and embrace the present, and welcome a brighter but different future—for you and your loved ones—forever!

I am standing upon the seashore.
A ship, at my side,
spreads her white sails
to the moving breeze
and starts for the blue ocean.

—Henry Van Dyke

ONE

Grief, Loss, and Time Perspective Therapy

Throughout our lifetimes, we—all human beings—will share a mysterious experience. Although the way in which it manifests is as unique as each one of us, and some will experience it more often than others, the event and aftermath will cause a flood of tremendous emotion and inescapable pain. It will rock our world, change the way we view our lives, tear our hearts open, and leave us devastated and changed forever. This often-overwhelming occurrence is universal in that every human being old enough to be fully conscious of what is important in their lives will know it at some point. This experience is the loss of someone precious to you, followed by grief.

In Western culture, grief has been a strange placeholder in the book of our lives. If we haven't experienced it before, we might expect grief to be finite—that we'll grieve for a certain amount of time. Then we'll "get over it" and return to "normal." But grief often lasts longer than we—or the people in our lives—thought it would. And if we're honest, maybe we never get over it. Maybe we shouldn't. Because grief isn't a placeholder. It's an ongoing process that is impossible for us to ignore. Instead, our loss should be acknowledged, accepted, and respected.

• • •

When our grief results from the loss of a loved one, it is usually thought to be a private and solitary experience. The death affects all the family members, friends, and others who knew the deceased. They each take their own path through their grief. It's intimate. It's personal.

Consider also the extreme experiences some of us may undergo—devastating incidents such as the ravages of war, horrifying terrorist attacks, catastrophic mass gun violence, and/or destructive natural disasters, like recurring tornadoes or flooding, in which many people are killed and their homes destroyed. These shared experiences culminate in what is called *collective* grief, which we'll explore later in this chapter.

The vehicle that brought collective grief to almost all human beings instantly appeared on our planet in late 2019 and early 2020, and it immediately commenced wrecking lives. It wasn't a manmade war, nor was it a terrorist attack. It was and continues to be severe acute respiratory syndrome coronavirus 2 (SARS-CoV-2), also known as COVID-19. This novel virus and its ever-mutating global spinoffs have affected humanity in many ways. COVID-19 has caused us to grieve for our losses and the unexpected changes it gave rise to, personally and collectively—losses that include, first and foremost, those who have died. But there are also the loss of jobs, restricted education, financial hardships, and the passing away of the life we once knew.

Fortunately, overall, we are recovering from the ravages of COVID-19. Unfortunately, gun-related mass murders continue to increase at an unbelievably rapid rate. As this book is written, in the United States, there have been more mass shootings than all the days that have passed in the year. Whenever these violent acts occur, numerous people are affected by the deaths and maiming of innocent children and adults.

When we add the growing number of natural catastrophes wrought by climate change—fires, floods, monster hurricanes, tornadoes, freezing temperatures in the winters followed by record-breaking heat in the summers—which bring with them death and destruction, we have a trio of disasters unique in our history. A trio that causes most of us and our nation to be frozen in constant mourning. And this doesn't even include the *personal* loss and grief we feel when a loved one passes on.

How can we overcome such pain, such heavy hearts? How can we move forward with our lives when we are constantly sad and depressed? Let's start by understanding exactly what we're experiencing when we grieve.

The Difference Between Grief, Mourning, and Loss

Grief is a necessary and incredibly important aspect of life for us to experience. It is generally associated with the death of a loved one, stillbirth, or miscarriage, but, as mentioned above, grief is also experienced when we lose something important to us, something that may have helped define us—perhaps a close relationship that we cherished or a job or career, including work relationships that helped describe who we are and that we considered a part of our personal identity. Let's also include the racial and social inequalities that have held us back from experiencing the civil rights enjoyed by some but not all; the education we did not, for whatever reason, complete; and the financial instability caused by forces beyond our control. We can also grieve for these social, political, and very personal hardships.

In *Seeing Through the Grief,* for the most part, when we refer to grief, we'll be referring to the loss of a loved one, a person or a special pet. However, the information and exercises we share can apply to any grief and loss experience, no matter what it encompasses.

Grief can bring with it feelings of abandonment, helplessness, and the pain of being separated, as well as a greater awareness of the fragility of our lives. Add in the fear of an unknown and different future than we had planned. In the earlier part of grief, a sense of deep loss is often experienced. As time progresses, emotions lessen but are still painful, and the feelings of permanent loss may appear as a separate part of our grieving process.

Although we tend to interchange the terms *grief* and *mourn,* or *grieving* and *mourning,* there are differences:

- *Grief and grieving* are internalized. They are what we think and feel, like sadness, regret, fear, or possibly even numbness.
- *Mourn and mourning* are externalized. It's the process we go through to adapt to the loss of the deceased. Mourning is when we cry, talk about the death, or perhaps journal about our experience. Memorial services and burials are also part of the mourning process. These are ways to share the pain and confusion we feel—internally—and with other people—externally.

In time, as our lives settle somewhat and we become more accustomed to our loss, the outward expressions of our grief—the mourning—lessen. But our internalized emotions—the grief itself—can last much longer. Depending on how devastating the loss was, and how it affected our lives, it's not unusual to experience a level of grief throughout the remainder of our lifetime. These feelings may be fleeting (just a few moments) or longer lasting (days or weeks), especially around important dates such as birthdays, holidays, or the anniversary of our loved one's death.

We feel loss as an emptiness in every facet of our lives. We can feel it physically, emotionally, and spiritually. Although not as severe as active grief, that sense of loss is always there, just under the surface, like a constant heartache. Perhaps the easiest example for us to understand is the loss suffered in the case of being widowed. The two people who had joined together to become a new, main identity—a couple—are forever changed with the death of one. The surviving person, now no longer part of the couple, suffers feelings of loss as they sort out who they are now, as a solitary soul, and how their life path will go on alone. The partner they spoke to, laughed with, tackled problems together and enjoyed life with is no longer there. Now they are alone, with only memories replacing the bonds of living and loving. But such loss is different from being lonely.

The Difference Between Loneliness and Being Alone

Loneliness is when you feel isolated. More than likely, it means you are in your own little inner world rather than the greater outside world. You might feel like an oddball, like you don't fit in, especially when others point out that you are widowed. Family, friends and acquaintances may not treat you as they did when you were part of a couple. (As an aside, some people seem to treat widowed men and women differently. Widowed men may be introduced to single women friends, while widowed women may be held in suspicion or viewed as a threat by other wives, causing deeper feelings of loneliness.)

Being alone is very different from feeling lonely. Being alone is not so much an emotion as a mindset. It's the realization that although your life has changed and you are no longer part of a couple, you can act, react, feel, and join in the world as an individual. Although it may feel scary, especially at first, the foundation that you helped build prior to your loss is strong enough to get you through this period all by yourself. This is being "alone."

But What Is Grief?

Grief is the powerful and often uncontrollable response people feel after a trauma or personally painful experience. It isn't just one emotion; it's multifaceted and affects us emotionally, mentally, physically, and spiritually. Grief is like post-trauma in that it can be deeply embedded in the brain and isn't located in any one domain. We know that our sight, smell, hearing, physical sensation or pain, and memories are all stored in different parts of the brain. Sad or painful thoughts can be triggered whenever one of these senses reminds us of our loss. During the grieving process, it's normal to feel deep sadness, apathy, and sometimes anger and guilt. In general, these negative feelings gradually lessen as the loss is accepted, which allows us to move forward with our new life.

We usually link grief to the loss of a loved one. But many other events can trigger grief to varying degrees. These can include the end of a relationship (marriage, friendship, or romantic) and traumatizing accidents or other near-death experiences. Also consider a serious illness or disease (whether yours or affecting a loved one), losing physical mobility or independence, a significant change in lifestyle or financial status, the loss of a job, or events that violate your feeling of security or safety, such as being robbed.

Each of us is a one-of-a-kind being, so it makes sense that we experience grief in our own unique way. Even if we experience the same or a similar loss, like the death of a parent, or child, or pet, the grief each family member experiences can vary widely from one person to another. Although we all experience grief throughout our lifetimes, there are different types of grief beyond what's considered normal or common grief.

What Is "Normal" or "Common" Grief?

After we've suffered a great loss, most people go through some or all of the following experiences temporarily while grieving in the subsequent days, weeks or months:

- *Tears*—crying or sobbing
- *Sleep pattern changes*—difficulty falling asleep or getting too little/ too much sleep
- *Lack of energy*—feeling lethargic or apathetic about the day's necessary tasks or life in general
- *Appetite changes*—loss of appetite or eating too much, particularly junk food
- *Withdrawal*—isolating from typical social interactions and relationships
- *Difficulty concentrating*—lack of focus on tasks, whether at work or home (hobbies, watching television, reading, and so forth)
- *Intensified feelings*—anger, guilt, loneliness, depression, sadness, emptiness, though still occasionally experiencing moments of joy and happiness
- *Questioning*—spiritual or religious beliefs, job or career choices, or your life goals

Gradually, in the weeks or months after our loss, we find our "new normal" life. We don't forget what caused our grief, but, in time, we learn to cope with the absence and the wound of our broken heart slowly begins to heal.

How Long Will I Mourn?

Simply put, there is no "normal" amount of time to grieve; the time frame is as individual as you. However, the length of your grieving process may depend on several things, such as your personality, age, beliefs, and support system. The type of loss can also help determine how long you grieve. For instance, you'll probably grieve longer over the death of a loved one than over the end of a relationship or loss of a job. It helps to understand your emotions and take care of yourself. Over time, the feelings of grief will lessen. You'll feel joy and happiness more frequently and be able to return to your life again.

Many Kinds of Grief

During our years of research, we discovered many different types of grief. After careful consideration, we have chosen nine that you or someone you know may experience at some point in your lives. Here they are in alphabetical order:

Abbreviated grief is a shortened response to a loss. It can occur when the void that was left by the loss is immediately filled by someone or something else or when one has experienced anticipatory grief (see below).

Absent grief is observed when a person shows only a few (or no) signs of anguish about the death of a loved one. This may be caused by denial or avoidance of the emotional realities of the loss. It may also happen if the deceased was ill, especially for some time, and the person who lost their loved one experienced anticipatory grief (see below). Or perhaps the loss hasn't sunk in yet, or even though the deceased may have been an immediate relative, the relationship wasn't close.

Anticipatory grief occurs before an impending loss. Usually, the loss is the expected death of someone we're close to due to illness; it can also be experienced by the dying person. However, life-altering surgeries (e.g., mastectomy, the loss of a limb, or heart surgery), the likelihood of the end of a relationship, business downsizing, or war can also cause anticipatory grief. In the first instance, one may feel heightened concern for the dying person, have recurring thoughts of their death, and ponder how their life will be affected once their loved one has passed. Anticipatory grief is an active process that differs from person to person.

While this interval might grant people time to settle issues with the dying person as well as bid them farewell, unfortunately, at the time of writing this book, anticipatory grief lacks social acceptance. And while some may experience closure before the loss, anticipatory grief doesn't generally replace post-loss grief. Since grief is different for each of us, the grief experienced before the loss doesn't necessarily reduce the grief after death. That said, for some people, there may be little post-loss grief due to anticipatory grief. In fact, they may feel relief.

When family members are caregivers during a loved one's dying process, they often find themselves increasingly protective of their loved one. This heightened need to protect may be part of the anticipatory grief experience in that the caregiver is trying to be with their loved one in the moment. (As an aside, the need to protect may also occur as their loved one comes closer to their death. It's normal for a person who is dying to not want to see some people in their greater circle. Instead, their focus may be on being with family members and those to whom they feel closest.) It's not unusual for anticipatory grief to cause additional stress and a decrease in physical and mental health. For this reason, it's helpful for those affected to seek support from each other as well as professionals involved in the loved one's care (i.e., hospice employees, social workers, and nurses).

Collective grief is experienced by a group of people, such as a community or nation, due to a natural or manmade disaster, terrorist attack, war, the death of a well-known person, or an event resulting in mass casualties or deaths, such as COVID-19. Collective grief can include feelings of loss of control, justice, identity and predictability. In some instances (such as a global pandemic), the losses are ambiguous. In other words, we don't know how or to what extent we'll be affected or for how long. In times like these, it's healthy to grieve for what's been lost so we can adapt and move forward. Like common grief, collective grief can cause periods of mourning and sadness as well as periods of acceptance and even happiness. Moving in and out of these feelings is more than okay, and it's actually good to distract yourself, experience joy, and laugh; doing so helps people cope with grief and loss.

Complicated grief poses a unique challenge. If grief becomes debilitating and symptoms such as painful emotions are so severe that you have trouble resuming your usual activities, you may be suffering from complicated, chronic, or prolonged grief. This heightened state of mourning interrupts the healing process. Some signs of complicated grief are:

- Intense sorrow and reflection on your loss
- Inability to focus on little except the loss of the deceased
- Intense and persistent longing for the loved one
- Problems accepting the death
- Numbness or detachment
- Bitterness about the loss
- Feeling that life holds no meaning or purpose
- Lack of trust in others
- Inability to enjoy life or think back on positive experiences with the loved one

Although the following symptoms are common during grief, if they continue for an extended period of time, they may indicate complicated grief:

- Difficulty carrying out normal routines
- Isolation from others and withdrawal from social activities
- Depression, deep sadness, guilt, or self-blame
- Belief that you did something wrong and/or could have prevented the death
- Feeling that life isn't worth living without your loved one
- Wishing you had died along with your loved one

While we don't know why some people suffer from complicated grief, it might be connected to environment, personality, inherited traits, and the body's natural chemicals.

Cumulative grief can occur when the grieving process isn't complete before another loss happens or when multiple losses occur at one time. It can also happen if a loss years earlier wasn't adequately dealt with (see *delayed grief*), which may cause the new loss to be overwhelming. Experiencing multiple losses in a short time can lead to complicated grief (see above). Avoidance may increase, along with the use of self-medication (alcohol, drugs) to numb the pain, which likewise delays grief. When such substance abuse is reduced or ceases, cumulative grief may become staggering. Elderly people may be more likely to suffer cumulative grief as relatives and people they know pass away more frequently than in their earlier life.

To integrate multiple losses into our lives, it's important to individually grieve each one, taking into consideration the relationship with that person, as well as the circumstances of their death. If one is religious or spiritual, cumulative grief can test one's faith. It can cause people to question why such a thing would occur or even strengthen their belief in a Higher Power. Either way, it is normal.

Delayed grief occurs when common grief is suspended but reappears later. Delayed grief isn't unusual after the death of a loved one due to the numerous things that need to be accomplished. Many people who've lost a loved one feel they must appear strong and tamp down their emotions to be a sturdy shoulder for others in their family. Keeping busy with projects and work is another common way for people to delay their grief process.

But the trouble is that if we suppress our emotional pain and ignore it, it doesn't go away. It just lurks deeper in our psyche, and it can work its way into other aspects of our lives. Delayed grief can have a negative impact on our health, causing headaches and stomach problems, as well as a myriad of other concerns. It can also ruin previously healthy social relationships. We've been trained in modern society to hide our emotions of grief and sorrow. We're told to buck up, to smile through the pain and sadness, to be "strong." It isn't any wonder that many of us find ourselves suffering from delayed grief.

Disenfranchised grief occurs when the loss is ignored or minimized by others, and it is often linked to cultural, societal or religious beliefs. In these instances, grief is minimized, experienced out of public view, and often disregarded. The societal stigma of suicide and drug overdose, whether intentional or not, may cause the mourner to experience disenfranchised grief. The mourner then feels they are not acknowledged, validated, or supported by society. If the mourner's relationship with the deceased is, for some reason, not recognized, the mourner can also experience disenfranchised grief.

Prolonged grief is a recognized disorder with distinct symptoms (intense longing for the deceased, difficulty accepting the loss, flattened affect and emotional numbness, confused identity, bitterness, an inability to trust others, feeling trapped by grief) that remain intense and are disabling for six months or more after the death. Mental health assistance is a necessity for those suffering from prolonged grief, as destructive behaviors and suicidal thoughts are common.

Is Depression a Part of Grief?

Yes, depression is a part of grief, especially since the most common symptom of depression is "feeling sad or empty for two or more weeks."

When we grieve, there is no magic wand waved a fortnight after our loss that miraculously takes away the pain or makes us forget what we've just experienced. Nor should we want to forget! Being depressed occasionally throughout our lifetime is part of the human experience. It's normal. And so is being depressed when someone we love has passed away. This type of depression is called "situational depression," as it is a specific situation—the death of a loved one—that is causing the depression.

According to our friends at the National Institute of Mental Health, "Depression (also called major depressive disorder or clinical depression) is a common but serious mood disorder. It causes severe symptoms that affect how you feel, think, and handle daily activities, such as sleeping, eating, or working. To be diagnosed with depression, the symptoms must be present for at least two weeks."

In other words, you may feel sad and have difficulty concentrating, your appetite may be affected, and you may sleep more and feel dejected. But in most cases, when we experience depression caused by grief, we won't require mental health therapy or medication. We realize that we'll get better over time.

When we're grieving, it's important to stay in touch with our feelings and know the signs if we're beginning to slip into a more serious depression. Major depression lasts a long time or reoccurs frequently. If you have some or all of the symptoms in the following list, you may suffer from major depression. If so, then we advise you to consider seeing a physician or mental health specialist for help as soon as possible.

Symptoms of major depression are:

- Feeling depressed, being sad to the point of tears and/or having an "empty" feeling. You can't hide feeling this depressed; people notice and probably ask whether you are okay.
- Losing interest and/or pleasure in the things you used to enjoy; you don't feel like doing any of the fun things you used to do.
- Isolating yourself from others; you prefer to be alone. You might eat your meals away from the family or stay home when others are going out.
- Experiencing significant weight loss when you aren't trying to lose weight or significant weight gain (more than 5 percent of body weight in a month).
- An inability to sleep well or sleeping excessively; it's hard to wake up when you are supposed to, and you never feel fully rested.
- Irritability and anger (irritability may also be a symptom in

children or adolescents): things that used to not bother you now irritate you often.

- Feeling fatigue or loss of energy; you don't have the "get up and go" you used to possess.
- Feeling worthless (I am no good to anybody, including myself) or excessively guilty (Why did I say that? What was I thinking?).
- Difficulty concentrating and/or thinking properly; you are unable to make decisions (I don't know what to do or which way to go).
- Recurring thoughts of death (the world would be a better place without me) or suicide without a specific plan (I want to kill myself, but I haven't thought of how I'd do it), or having a plan to commit suicide (I want to kill myself, and I know exactly how I'd do it), or even making a suicide attempt.

We can't emphasize enough that feeling depressed during the grieving process is normal. However, if you're experiencing thoughts of death or suicide, we urge you to seek help right away. Call someone you're close to and tell them how you feel. Or, if you are in the United States, call 988—the National Suicide and Crisis Lifeline. Twenty-four hours a day, seven days a week, there are people available who care about you and want to help you get past this ominous time in your life.

Is Anxiety a Part of Grief?

Anxiety is not necessarily a part of the grieving process; it depends on your experience, your situation, and possibly your personality or state of mind. In simple terms, anxiety is an intense fear or worry that something bad is going to happen in the future—anywhere from a few seconds or minutes away to much further down the road. The National Institute of Mental Health defines anxiety as "intense, excessive, and persistent worry and fear about everyday situations. Fast heart rate, rapid breathing, sweating, and feeling tired may occur. Anxiety can be normal in stressful situations such as public speaking or taking a test."

In the case of grief and anxiety, we discovered in our interviews of widowed people that worrying about finances could be cause for anxiety, especially if the deceased spouse was the chief income-earner. These widowed people felt insecure about whether their financial needs would be met, even if their spouse had made provisions for them. One widow told us, "My husband had a business that basically runs itself, and he had an insurance policy, plus I can collect his Social Security survivors' benefits.

But I'm constantly worried that it'll all be taken away and I'll be homeless." This thought—"that I'll be homeless"—was shared by other widowed people, even when logically their fear would never come to fruition.

To be clear, it's not unusual to feel anxious or worried during the grieving process. But it's a good idea to monitor how worried you are, and if you feel like it's becoming extreme, then it's time to talk to a professional. After reading the following list, if you recognize having some or all of the symptoms, you may suffer from generalized anxiety disorder. If so, then we advise you to consider seeing a physician or mental health specialist for help as soon as you can.

Generalized anxiety usually involves a persistent feeling of anxiety or dread, which can interfere with daily life. It is not the same as occasionally worrying about things or experiencing anxiety due to stressful life events. People living with generalized anxiety experience frequent anxiety for months, if not years.

Symptoms of generalized anxiety are as follows (note that some are the same as major depression):

- Feeling restless, wound up, or on edge
- Being easily fatigued
- Having difficulty concentrating
- Being irritable
- Having headaches, muscle aches, stomachaches, or unexplained pains
- Difficulty controlling feelings of worry
- Having sleep problems, such as difficulty falling or staying asleep

In our work with grieving people, some described a phenomenon that overcame them instantly and seemingly out of nowhere: they thought they were having a heart attack or were afraid they were dying. In some instances, paramedics were called, or the mourning person was taken to the emergency room. After being thoroughly checked, each was told they had suffered a *panic attack*. Panic attacks are associated with anxiety. Many people have one or two panic attacks in their lifetimes; that's it, and the problem goes away, more than likely when a stressful situation ends. Although panic attacks themselves aren't life-threatening, they can be frightening and significantly affect your quality of life. If they are recurrent and cause you to spend long periods in fear of another attack, you may have panic disorder. However, it's important to know that not everyone who has a panic attack develops panic disorder. Nevertheless, it is good to know panic attack symptoms:

- Pounding or racing heart
- Sweating
- Trembling or tingling
- Chest pain
- Feelings of impending doom
- Feelings of being out of control

In extreme circumstances, panic attacks can occur several times a day, or they may occur as rarely as a few times a year (or less). If you feel you have panic disorder, please see your physician as soon as possible.

Is Stress a Part of Grief?

Yes, stress is part of the grieving process. We've all been stressed from time to time. But what *is* stress? According to the National Institute of Mental Health, stress "is the physical or mental response to an external cause, such as having a lot of homework or having an illness. A stressor may be a one-time or short-term occurrence, or it can happen repeatedly over a long time." According to the Holmes and Rahe Stress Scale, the death of a spouse—and, we add, child—is the most stressful event a person experiences in life. (As an aside, you can take the Holmes and Rahe Stress test online at *https://www.test-stress.com/en/stress-tests.php.*)

Here are some facts concerning stress provided by the National Institute of Mental Health with our input about loss and grief:

- Generally, stress is a response to an external cause, such as taking a big test or arguing with a friend or grieving the death of a loved one, which is life altering.
- Stress goes away once the situation is resolved. In the case of losing a loved one, the stress dissipates over time as we learn to cope with our loss.
- Stress can be positive or negative. For example, it may inspire you to meet a deadline, or it may cause you to lose sleep. When we are mourning, the stress we feel will more than likely be negative. However, it can also cause us to accomplish necessary things we don't feel like doing; of course, even then, it's hard to consider the stress "positive."

Like depression and anxiety, stress can affect your mind and body. You may experience symptoms such as:

- Excessive worry
- Uneasiness
- Tension
- Headaches or body pain
- High blood pressure
- Loss of sleep

By knowing what causes your stress, you have taken one giant step forward in learning how to cope with your grief and are now looking ahead, toward your path to a more positive future.

• • •

Religions and Spiritual Practices: How We Mourn—Part 1

In each chapter, we'll share information about how humans have mourned throughout time and around the globe. We'll cover the major religions as well as some of the spiritual beliefs of the Original or Indigenous Peoples in Africa, the Americas, Australia and Polynesia. With deep reverence, we hope to gain a better understanding of the many ways humans view death and how we grieve.

According to archeological evidence, the earliest practice of burial discovered so far is about 130,000 years old. This is when we find that Neanderthals practiced burying their dead. The bodies—some positioned as if they were sleeping—were discovered with goods, including piles of ancient pollen, which are the remains of flowers, suggesting proper burials associated with the belief in an afterlife. At one site that's estimated to be 50,000 years old, four bodies were found in a cluster with an abundance of pollen. So we can surmise that Neanderthals, who lived in groups of ten to thirty people, grasped the concept that when one in their group died, whatever it was that animated that member had disappeared, leaving behind the physical body, which then began to decay. This, we believe for all intents and purposes, is the start of experiencing spiritual beliefs.

Since then, spiritual practices and religions have offered a deep and layered tradition of how to care for and prepare the body, rites to follow, prayers to assist departed loved ones on their journey beyond this world, and ways to honor the deceased at home in the days to come. Equally important, these traditions help those in mourning cope with their loss. The dictates regarding periods of mourning vary according to religion, culture, and current socially accepted expressions of grief.

But before we share information we've gathered about grief and mourning in major world religions, we'd like to note a growing occurrence in the United States about what some may call "nonbelievers" (or "nones").

ATHEISTS AND AGNOSTICS

The label "nonbelievers" refers to those who check the nonaffiliation box on surveys about religions. According to research reported by Michael Shermer in *Scientific American*, in 2015, almost 25 percent of the American participants in a study identified as being atheists or agnostic. To put this finding into perspective, just eight years earlier, in 2007, this number was 16 percent. Additionally, many people have pulled away from mainstream religions into what may be considered New Age spiritual movements. This development is evident from two *Pew* polls cited by Shermer, one of which was conducted in 2012 among people who reported being spiritual but not religious. At that time, the number was 19 percent. In the second poll, taken just five years later in 2017, the reported number increased to 27 percent.

Interestingly, among some atheists and agnostics, one of the most important facets of religious faith has carried over into what was once a strictly nonspiritual belief. For instance, as Shermer notes, an Austin Institute for the Study of Family and Culture survey conducted in 2014 found that of the 13.2 percent identifying as atheist or agnostic, 32 percent answered in the affirmative when asked "Do you think there is life, or some sort of conscious existence, after death?" Although the survey stopped there and didn't query further to get to the root beliefs of these folks, Shermer suspects these nonbelievers have "adopted … New Age notions of the continuation of consciousness without brains via some kind of 'morphic resonance' or quantum field (or some such)."

Now, let's look at a few specifics regarding death and grieving in some of the world's largest religions and the spiritual practices of major Indigenous cultures. In our research into worldwide grief and mourning practices, we were astonished to discover that there are thousands of religions or sects as well as Indigenous cultures, many of which varied in their practices. What we learned would make—for some—an interesting and lengthy book, but that is not the intent of *this* book. So we chose to go with Pew Research Center's work regarding religions, in which five major religions are considered. These five are, in order, according to the number of their worldwide followers, Christianity, Islam, Buddhism, Hinduism, and Judaism. However, we present these religions here in alphabetical order.

The next group of religions is presented in Chapter Two and the last in Chapter Three. The mourning practices and some spiritual beliefs of major Indigenous cultures are shared in Chapter Four.

Buddhism

The Buddhist religion is a worldwide spiritual practice, with variation in custom and ritual from one sect to another. Many have a more intense period of mourning in which prayers, chants and rituals are performed in the home on the seventh day, the forty-ninth day and the one hundredth day after the death of a member. Or some may choose the seventh-day, the three-month and the one-year anniversaries. The dates are not as important as the gathering of family to hold simple services and share a spiritual experience in the memories honoring their loved one. While there are no set times restricting normal activities such as work, many Buddhist sects discourage a return to social activities during a ninety-day period of mourning. In certain strands of Asian Buddhism, there are lesser rituals that may continue for a one-year period, during which time the bereaved should wear only the traditional white or the acceptably adapted Western black attire. The wealth of Buddhist practices offers many traditions, including the Kamidana-fuji (house shrine), which is used for thirty-five days after the passing of a family member, said to keep the home pure even when the power of death reigns over it. The seven days following the death are the time for others to visit the family following a practice known as "merit transfer," in which gifts of virtue and prayers are offered on behalf of the deceased. This practice brings comfort and support to the family and increases the good energy and karma of the transitioning spirit, generating positive circumstances for rebirth.

• • •

The Elephant in the Room

Many of us don't know what to do, how to act, or what to say when we're around people who are grieving. People might skirt around the subject, or leap over it, but many will ignore it. They know "it's" there and that you're going through "something." But unless they've experienced loss, they might not know what to say or how to behave. And sometimes even if they *have* endured something similar, their actual experience may be very different from yours. This difference may cause them to slip back into old ways or freeze up because *your* loss brings back memories of *their* loss. These are the ingredients for awkward and sometimes unintended but hurtful social moments.

Most people will want to show support and sympathize with you. For a variety of reasons, they'll say things—sometimes obvious things—that they think are helpful. Perhaps they don't know any other way, or they think you may not have thought about what they want to tell you, or they've heard other people say something similar:

They are in a better place.
They lived a long life.
At least they aren't suffering anymore.
It was their time.
God called them home.

You probably recognize some of these sentiments, and perhaps in the past you've said them to others who have lost a loved one.

We seem to automatically know what to say and do and how to act during happy conditions, like when a baby is born or when we attend a birthday celebration or a wedding. We probably even know what to say during difficult times like the loss of a job or end of a relationship. But for some reason we have the hardest time when the saddest of sad things happen and people we know have lost a loved one and are grieving. We can blame this situation as a failing on the part of society, or we can take responsibility and be more conscious of what's happening and how our words affect others for better or for worse.

The Unkindest Things
to Say to a Mourner

We're including this section for anyone who may be nervous or at a loss for words in this situation. We'd like to make sure they *don't* say these things. These are also pro tips from psychologist and professor at Tulane Medical School Department of Psychiatry, Marilyn Mendoza, for people in the field of mental health to help guide their clients.

Most articles on the subject of what to say to the bereaved suggest readers not worry because the mourner will automatically understand that they're coming from a place of love and caring. Not true. We know this because grief counselors frequently hear about "well-meaning" comments that have actually offended or angered the mourner. So, please, do not say:

- You need to put this behind you.
- It was not meant to be.
- I thought you would be more upset.
- He brought this on himself.
- Everything happens for a reason.
- It is not good to visit the grave so often.
- Others have it worse than you.
- Are you over her yet? She's been gone a long time.
- You must be strong.
- You know that he cannot get into heaven until you accept his death.
- Why are you still crying?
- She wouldn't want you to be so sad.
- If you separate his ashes, he will never get to heaven.
- You are still young; you can always remarry.
- You never really got to know the baby.
- At least the other twin lived.
- God wanted him more than you.
- Heaven needed another angel.
- God will never give you more than you can handle.
- I know just how you feel.
- Don't let the children see your sadness.
- You do have other children.

These comments may seem very different, but they are all similar in that they are *judgmental* and *controlling*. Making comments such as these may indicate our own discomfort with the situation, so we try to minimize others' grief or "fix" it for ourselves and them, which unfortunately only makes things worse.

Here are some additional "don'ts" we've learned from grief counselors about things that are inappropriate or may be upsetting to a mourner:

- *If you can't attend the funeral, memorial or celebration of life, don't mention why.* The only reason good enough for the person/people whose life/lives have been changed forever is if one of your loved ones recently passed away.
- *Don't try to distract a mourner from their grief.* It may be in your nature to "fix" other people or their problems, but they don't need fixing. Right now, they need time and space.
- *Don't insist that you know how they are feeling right now.* It's okay to say that you've "been there," but only if you really have, and

don't assume that you know what they're going through because only they know what they are experiencing.

- *Don't assume they're okay.* They might appear to be fine or say they are when asked, but they may be struggling.
- *Don't make their grief about you.* No matter who they've lost, don't share stories of your grandparent's or pet's demise. It's not at all helpful.
- *Read the room before you decide to be overly humorous or tell jokes.* Sometimes a funny story can be healing, but at other times it can bring tears of sadness when the mourner realizes their vibrant loved one is gone. Tread lightly.
- *Don't encourage mourners to be stoic.* "Hang in there," "be brave," and "keep a stiff upper lip" are statements that can discourage the release of emotion, which is a healthy part of the grieving process.
- *Don't remind them that life goes on.* Although it's true, when grief is fresh, that's not the time to say it.
- *Don't use clichés, including religious platitudes.* Even if the person grieving is religious, more than likely right now there's no place they'd rather have their loved one than by their side.

Fortunately, mourners have confirmed that there are helpful and compassionate things you *can* say to help them with their grief. So, if you're trying to comfort a grieving person, consider saying one or more of the following:

- I don't know how you feel, but I am here to help in whatever way you need me.
- I am sorry for your loss.
- I wish I had the right words to say. Just know I care.
- I am sorry you have to go through this.
- I will keep you and your loved one in my thoughts and prayers.
- I am just a phone call away.
- I'm bringing dinner over.

These helpful acknowledgments are neither judgmental nor controlling. They are supportive and don't tell the mourner what to think, do, or feel, nor do they try to fix an irreparable situation. After a death, there may be a slew of people around the mourner. But after a few weeks or a couple of months, when others have returned to their normal lives, a grieving person may feel deserted. What can you do? Stay in touch, call or text them periodically, give them a hug when you see them, ask how they're doing, listen to what they have to say, and cry with them if you are also on the verge of tears. We can help the most by being there and being supportive.

Here are a few more suggestions to say out loud or in a condolence note when the time is right. Please note that your sincerity is the essential ingredient:

- *Speak the deceased person's name.* Saying the name of the person who has passed on is comforting and validates the mourner's grief. Using the present tense, especially shortly after the loved one has passed, is perfectly acceptable (for instance, "Brian is greatly missed" or "Mary is always in my thoughts/prayers/heart"). Sadly, some family and friends will ignore the situation and act as if the deceased never existed. This reaction can be very confusing and hurtful for the bereaved. We believe this can happen when those family and friends are ignorant about grief and grieving or have been taught that it is unacceptable or inappropriate to acknowledge grief or sadness or that it is a sign of weakness, or perhaps they feel grief is so private that they should not interfere with the bereaved person's process. Whatever their reason, it's wrong to act that way.
- *Be sincere.* The way we say things matters almost as much as what we say. "I'm sorry for your loss," which the mourner will probably hear scores of times, means so much more when the tone of voice is genuine. It can also be very soothing.
- *Let them know you'll check on them.* Grief doesn't end after the funeral. You can show the grieving person how much you care by sending them a text message, email, or note that you'll be in touch in a week or two, or as soon as they're up to it. Consider bringing them a meal. Then follow through.
- *Tell them they are loved.* This can be in person or in written form. Convey how much you love them and the person who died. For instance, "I love you, and I love and miss Brian, too," or "I love you; you and Mary have always meant the world to me."
- *Share a favorite memory.* Use your discernment to determine when the time might be right, and when you feel it is, share a past positive memory or two of the deceased. The bereaved may or may not have heard the story before. This can bring comfort or a new perspective of their loved one or your relationship with their loved one, which can be appreciated and enjoyed.

• • •

Now we'll directly address the mourner: If you are grieving, you may want to go ballistic on the unlucky person who utters the rote saying that becomes the proverbial straw that breaks your camel's back. But please, please, please, stop before you say or do anything. We know you are in a very difficult place, and it's a lot to ask of you, but take a moment to muster your compassion and know that this person means well; they just don't understand how their words affect you. Assume they meant well but screwed up. Take a deep breath. Exhale. Maybe look at the ground if you can't look them in the eye. And nod. That's it. Just nod. You don't have to say anything.

Some say death is the great equalizer. But perhaps grief is as well, because, at some point, we will all experience the pain and suffering of losing a family member, friend, or beloved pet. None of us gets a pass. If during the most trying of times we keep our wits about us and are kind, compassionate, and caring, we can turn a potentially tricky or hurtful situation into a positive learning experience for all.

What If I Need Help?

Sometimes our grief doesn't let up. We may be unable to accept the loss, and our "normal" grief may be much more complicated (see the discussion of complicated grief earlier in this chapter). It's important to talk to your doctor if you're experiencing the following symptoms for a prolonged length of time:

- Trouble keeping up your normal routine, like going to work or doing household chores
- Feelings of deep depression
- Thoughts that life isn't worth living or of harming yourself
- Inability to stop blaming yourself

A therapist can help you explore your emotions and teach you coping skills beyond this book to aid you in managing your grief. If you're depressed or anxious, a doctor might suggest an antidepressant or antianxiety medication for a while.

When we're in deep emotional pain, we may be tempted to try to numb these feelings with drugs, alcohol, food, or even work. But be careful. These are temporary escapes that won't make you heal faster or feel better in the long run. They can lead down the path to addiction, depression, anxiety, or an emotional breakdown.

In addition to following the suggestions in this book, remember to do these things:

- *Give yourself time.* Accept your feelings and know that grieving is a process.
- *Talk to others.* Spend time with friends and family; don't isolate yourself.
- *Take care of yourself.* Exercise regularly, eat well, and try to get enough sleep to stay healthy and energized.
- *Return to your hobbies.* Get back to the activities that bring you joy.
- *Join a support group.* Speak with others who are also grieving; it can help you feel more connected.

In addition, Happify (*happify.com*) offers a free four-week grief track with activities especially developed for you by the authors of this book.

Take This Quiz

Phil Zimbardo, along with his then graduate student John Boyd, developed the Zimbardo Time Perspective Inventory (ZTPI) in 1999 by using focus groups, interviewing many people from different walks of life, conducting surveys of thousands of people of all ages and then repeatedly refining the findings. The ZTPI is reliable in that it repeatedly gets consistent results and has proven to be valid, as it predicts a range of other traits and behaviors. It's the tool we've used to determine whether one's time perspective(s) might be too heavily weighted—that is, biased—and need to be balanced.

To get accurate results, it's best to take the ZTPI *before* you read the time perspective descriptions that follow the quiz. However, if you choose to take it after you've read further in this book, try to answer each of the statements as you would have done before reading ahead. Each item has to do with *past negative*, *past positive*, *present fatalism*, *present hedonism* or *future* time perspectives.

The following is the fifteen-item short form of the ZTPI so you can discover your personal time perspectives. Although the short form has proved to be accurate, you may also want to take the complete fifty-six-item ZTPI by going online to www.thetimeparadox.com/surveys/. It will be automatically scored for you.

While online, you'll find that Phil and his colleagues have developed a separate questionnaire to determine a sixth time perspective, the Transcendental-future Time Perspective Inventory. They decided to create this shorter quiz rather than tack it on to the ZTPI, in part because the complete ZTPI is lengthy. In a nutshell, transcendental-future-oriented people believe that life after death is more important than the life they are living. They may invest heavily in the afterlife during their current lifetime (as seen with the ancient Egyptians and the extensive pyramids they built).

During the development of time perspective therapy, we discovered that a significant number of research participants and clients had no religious affiliation, did not consider themselves spiritual, and did not believe in an afterlife. However, all research participants and clients wanted to improve their lives in the present and work toward a better future in their lifetimes. This being the case, the Transcendental-future Time Perspective Inventory is not used in time perspective therapy. However, religion, spirituality and culture are important factors in the grieving process and are summarized throughout this book.

Note: See Appendix I for the complete 56-item ZTPI.

• • •

When you have finished, use the scale below and follow the scoring rules. You will have a set of five scores that represent the degree to which each time perspective factors into your makeup. Using the ZTPI graph provided in Appendix I, take a moment to plot your scores on the graph. You'll notice that the ZTPI graph contains the ideal time perspective scores. When you compare your numerical score to the ideal, the result is a sense of how high or low you are in each area. In this way you can determine how your life experiences have contributed to your unique time perspective inventory profile. The power of this measuring tool is evident in that it has been translated into more than thirty languages worldwide and dozens of researchers from many nations have found significant effects using it in a host of research projects.

Zimbardo Time Perspective Inventory (ZTPI) Short Form

Read each item and, as honestly as you can, answer the statement: How characteristic or true is this of me? Please score all the statements according to the following scale:

1 (Very Untrue), 2 (Untrue), 3 (Neutral),
4 (True) and 5 (Very True)

1. I think about the bad things that have happened to me in the past.
2. Painful past experiences keep being replayed in my mind.
3. It's hard for me to forget unpleasant images of my youth.

4. Familiar childhood sights, sounds, smells often bring back a flood of wonderful memories.

5. Happy memories of good times spring readily to mind.

6. I enjoy stories about how things used to be in the "good old times."

7. Life today is too complicated; I would prefer the simpler life of the past.

8. Since whatever will be will be, it doesn't really matter what I do.

9. Often luck pays off better than hard work.

10. I make decisions on the spur of the moment.

11. Taking risks keeps my life from becoming boring.

12. It is important to put excitement in my life.

13. When I want to achieve something, I set goals and consider specific means for reaching those goals.

14. Meeting tomorrow's deadlines and doing other necessary work comes before tonight's play.

15. I complete projects on time by making steady progress.

Past negative: 1, 2, 3; Past positive: 4, 5, 6; Present fatalism: 7, 8, 9; Present hedonism: 10, 11, 12; Future: 13, 14, 15

Your highest score indicates your primary time perspective. Conversely, your lowest score indicates the time perspective you do not relate to very much or at all—depending on how low your score is. If you assigned the number 3 to all or the majority of the items, then perhaps you are anxious about taking a quiz or having to make a decision. Consider retaking the ZTPI at a later date to see whether your scores have changed. But in most cases, we've found that one score is highest and another score lowest. Although every score is important in determining your overall time perspective, the one or two highest scores and the one or two lowest scores will help determine why you behave the way you do. This knowledge enables you to balance primary negative time perspectives with positive time perspectives (if needed) and improve your overall time perspective. Remember: This information is for you. No one is judging you, and you might be surprised at how spot on the results are, especially after you read the following assessments.

Note: As grief and loss are generally considered situational experiences, and symptoms can lessen over time, keep in mind that your test results indicate your *current* time perspectives. Once you have completed reading this book and have implemented the suggestions for a while, we suggest you take the ZTPI again to see whether you have developed a brighter outlook.

• • •

Five Main Time Perspectives in Time Perspective Therapy

1. *Past positive*–oriented people focus on the "good old days." They look forward to celebrating traditional holidays, like to keep souvenirs from past experiences, and collect photos; they may have friends they've known since childhood.

2. *Past negative*–oriented people focus on what went wrong in the past. They live in a world of regrets and what could have been. They have a pessimistic view of their lives and the world; many past negative people prefer to think of themselves as "realists"—they believe the way they view the world is "the true" reality.

3. *Present hedonistic*–oriented people live in the moment. Their goals in life are to seek pleasure, sensation, and new and unique experiences; present hedonists frequently do this to avoid pain and may have addictive personalities.

4. *Present fatalistic*–oriented people feel that their fate is predetermined. Their destiny—and future—is set; they believe that they have little or no control over what happens to them and that their actions don't make a difference in the world. For some, this time perspective comes from their religious orientation; for others, it comes from a realistic assessment of their poverty or living with extreme hardships.

5. *Future*-oriented people are always thinking ahead. This trait can lean positive or negative. In the positive, future-oriented people plan for the future and trust in their decisions. In the extreme, or negative, they may become workaholics, leaving little time to enjoy or appreciate what they have worked so hard to achieve. But whether they lean positive or negative, future-oriented people are most likely to succeed in their careers and not get in trouble.

A Balanced Time Perspective Leads to Greater Stability

The goal of this book is twofold: to help people going through the grieving process identify their time perspectives and to guide them in learning to balance their past, present and future time perspectives to once again live happier, more meaningful lives. The added bonus to achieving a balanced time perspective is *stability*. You may ask, "How does this work?" Well, a person's mindset is "unbalanced" or "unstable" when their main focus is a negative time perspective—for example, *past negative* (constantly thinking about the bad things that happened); *present fatalism* (unable to get out of the funk of thinking life is horrible and we are all doomed); extreme *present hedonism* (constantly seeking pleasure or a steady adrenaline rush at the expense of the future); or extreme *future oriented* to the point of missing out on the good things happening now. In the context of this book, we mean "unbalanced" or "unstable" in the sense that a negative time perspective mindset may cause a person to make unwise decisions or not optimize their life situations and relationships.

If you take a ten-thousand-foot-high view of our world, you'll note that the vast majority of the people you see every day—the person trying to comfort you but really seeking comfort for him-/herself, the always-in-a-hurry supervisor too busy to acknowledge you, the disgruntled customer in the checkout line, the homeless person sitting on the curb asking you for change, the driver of the car honking their horn and riding your bumper on the freeway, the teenager who knows it all—may have unbalanced time perspectives and don't know it. Why? Because we take time for granted and don't realize how precious and important it is until it runs out.

When we practice the simple techniques outlined in this book, when we take the time to set aside our grief for a little while in order to view our past, present and future (and make adjustments if and when they are needed), then we gain stability in the very core of our being. We handle situations better by understanding ourselves and others. We become more compassionate. We learn self-soothing coping skills by slowing down our breathing when we start to feel anxious and know that we can create a brighter future. We will relearn how to enjoy life more fully and thereby gain a more stable frame of mind as well as a more robust way of viewing life—and, eventually, we'll decide how to make each day the best it can be for us, forever.

Positive Effects

When our time perspectives are balanced, we can use our imaginations in wonderful ways. We can make peace with the past. We can reconnect and enjoy our time in the present with family and friends. And we can envision a brighter, more positive future that spans beyond our lifetime and leaves a legacy for those who follow us. Through our study of seasoned war veterans suffering from chronic and severe post-traumatic stress disorder (PTSD), as well as working with many hundreds of clients from varied backgrounds who came to us because of stress, depression, anxiety, life's many adjustments, or having lost a loved one, we've learned that not only is TPT very effective immediately, but it also has long-lasting benefits.

On a personal note, both authors are intimately familiar with the loss of loved ones. So we are all walking together on this special journey.

To Sum Up

- Grief and mourning are necessary and important aspects of being human. Grief is the powerful and often uncontrollable response people feel after a trauma or personally painful experience.
- Grief isn't just one emotion; it's multifaceted and affects us mentally, physically, and spiritually.
- Grief can bring with it feelings of abandonment and helplessness, the pain of being separated, a greater awareness of how fragile life is, and fear of an unknown and different future than we had planned.
- Mourning is the process we go through during grief.
- We feel loss as an emptiness in our lives. Loss can be felt physically, emotionally, and spiritually. Although not as severe as grief, it's always there, just under the surface, like a constant heartache.
- Loneliness is when you feel isolated; more than likely, it means you are in your own little world rather than the greater world around you.
- Being alone is not so much an emotion as a mindset. It's the realization that although your life has changed, you can act, react, feel, and join in the world as an individual. The foundation you helped build prior to your loss is strong enough to get you through by yourself.
- There are many types of grief other than "common" or "normal" grief, such as anticipatory grief, collective grief, complicated grief, cumulative grief, and delayed grief, as well as several others.
- It's normal to experience depression, stress and, on occasion, anxiety during the grieving process.
- The ZTPI can help determine whether your mindset is mostly in the past (negative or positive), present (fatalistic or hedonistic), or future.

- When you know your main time perspectives, and especially if they're skewed toward the negative, it's possible to learn to balance your past, present and future time perspectives in order to live a happier, more meaningful life.
- Achieving a balanced time perspective creates stability in your life.

REFERENCES

Eagleman, D. (2011). *Incognito: The secret lives of the brain*. New York, NY: Vintage.

Haley, E. (2020). Absent grief: Why am I not grieving like I expected to? *What's Your Grief*. https://whatsyourgrief.com/absent-grief-why-am-i-not-grieving-like-i-expected-to/.

Haley, E., & Williams, L. (2018, July 30). 17 types of grief every funeral director should know. *Funeral Friend*. http://thefuneralfriend.com/index.php/2018/07/30/17-types-of-grief-every-funeral-director-should-know/.

Harvard Medical School. (2022). *A guide to getting through grief*. Boston, MA: Harvard Health Publishing. https://www.health.harvard.edu/blog_extra/a-guide-to-getting-through-grief.

Holmes and Rahe Stress Scale. (n.d.), .https://www.test-stress.com/en/stress-tests.php.

Juan, S. (2006, October 6). What are the most widely practiced religions in the world? *The Register*. https://www.theregister.com/2006/10/06/the_odd_body_religion/.

Maciejewski, P.K., Zhang, B., Block, S., & Prigerson, H. (2007). An empirical examination of the stage theory of grief. *Journal of the American Medical Association, 297*(7), 716–23.

Mark, J. (2009, September 2). Burial. *World History Encyclopedia*. https://www.worldhistory.org/burial/.

Mayo Clinic Staff. (2016, October 19). What is grief? *Mayo Clinic*. https://www.mayoclinic.org/patient-visitor-guide/support-groups/what-is-grief.

Mayo Clinic Staff. (2022, December 13). Complicated grief. *Mayo Clinic*. https://www.mayoclinic.org/diseases-conditions/complicated-grief/symptoms-causes/syc-20360374.

Mendoza, M. (2016, June 17). The worst things to say to someone who's mourning. *Psychology Today*. https://www.psychologytoday.com/us/blog/the-guest-room/201606/the-worst-things-say-someone-whos-mourning.

Moore, M., & Lorenz, L. (2022). Mourning vs. grief: What's the difference? *Psych Central*. https://psychcentral.com/health/mourning-vs-grief.

Moralis, S., & Dinan, S. (2022, July 12). What not to say to someone dealing with a loss. *Psychology Today*. https://www.psychologytoday.com/us/blog/the-therapeutic-perspective/202207/what-not-say-someone-dealing-loss.

National Cancer Institute. (2022). Grief, bereavement, and coping with loss. *National Institute of Health*. https://www.cancer.gov/about-cancer/advanced-cancer/caregivers/planning/bereavement-hp-pdq#section/all.

NIMH Staff. (n.d.). Anxiety. *National Institute of Mental Health*. https://www.nimh.nih.gov/health/topics/anxiety-disorders.

NIMH Staff. (n.d.). Depression. *National Institute of Mental Health*. https://www.nimh.nih.gov/health/topics/depression.

NIMH Staff. (n.d.). I'm so stressed out. *National Institute of Mental Health*. https://www.nimh.nih.gov/health/publications/so-stressed-out-fact-sheet.

Papa, A., & Maitoza, R. (2013). The role of loss in the experience of grief. *Journal of Loss and Trauma, 18*(2). https://psycnet.apa.org/record/2012-33760-005.

Rando, T.A. (1986). *Loss and anticipatory grief*. Lanham, MD: Lexington Books.

Roy, K. (2019). Disenfranchised grief: When grief and grievers are unrecognized. *The New Social Worker*. https://www.socialworker.com/feature-articles/practice/disenfranchised-grief-when-grief-and-grievers-are-unrecogniz/.

Shermer, M. (2018). The number of Americans with no religious affiliation is rising. *Scientific American*. https://www.scientificamerican.com/article/the-number-of-americans-with-no-religious-affiliation-is-rising/.

Stroebe, M.S., Hansson, R.O., Schut, H., & Stroebe, W. (2008). *Handbook of bereavement research and practice: Advances in theory and intervention*. Washington, D.C.: American Psychological Association.

Stroebe, M.S., Hansson, R.O., Stroebe, W., & Schut, H. (2001). *Handbook of bereavement research: Consequences, coping, and care*. Washington, D.C.: American Psychological Association.

Than, K. (2013). Neanderthal burials confirmed as ancient ritual. *National Geographic*. https://www.nationalgeographic.com/culture/article/131216-la-chapelle-neanderthal-burials-graves.

Weir, K. (2020). Grief and COVID-19: Mourning our bygone lives. *American Psychological Association*. https://www.apa.org/news/apa/2020/04/grief-covid-19.

Zimbardo, P., & Boyd, J. (2008). *The time paradox: The new psychology of time that will change your life*. London, UK: Rider.

Zimbardo, P., & Sword, R.K.M. (2017). *Living and loving better: Healing from the past, embracing the present, creating an ideal future with time perspective therapy*. Jefferson, NC: McFarland.

I stand and watch her until, at length,
she hangs like a speck of white cloud
just where the sea and sky
come to mingle with each other.

—Henry Van Dyke

Two

The Past

When we think of the past, whether we're recalling a personal experience or something we've seen (like a film) or heard (like a podcast) or learned (from reading or schooling), sometimes it can be as if we're retelling a factual story to ourselves or maybe playing a scene in our mind. Let's try this right now. You can visualize a short story of your recent past by thinking of the last meal you ate. What was the time of day? Where were you? What did you eat? Did you or someone you know prepare the meal? If so, how did that come about? Were you alone, with someone else, or in a group? We could continue by asking whether your meal was on a plate or in a bowl, and so on, but you get the idea. Please take a moment to think about this setting.

If nothing comes to mind because you are in such deep grief or depression that you can't remember the last time you ate, *please stop*, put this book or tablet down, and get something to eat right now. We aren't going anywhere. We will wait for you. When you come back, you can pick up from **HERE**: Okay. If you remembered your last meal, we're pretty sure you were able to re-create the scene in detail and even remember the taste, smell and texture of the food. When life is normal, this is how we remember: factually.

But when we have experienced an event that is surprising or unpleasant, or when it violates our basic expectations—like the sudden loss of a loved one—and especially if it was in any way traumatic for us, our brain naturally formulates an account that describes what happened and why. This account may or may not be factual. By doing this, we're trying to make sense of what occurred. If the story isn't completely factual, it may be because of anxiety, or perhaps we can't process what actually happened yet. The story we tell ourselves is called a "narrative." When we're young, we have fewer memories and fewer skills or cognitive tools to create a coherent narrative. As we age, we gain causal coherence (the ability to describe experiences in sequence) and thematic coherence (the ability to identify underlying values and patterns that recur throughout the story).

Such narratives help us find meaning in our lives, and especially in our losses, which in turn facilitates healing.

We'll be digging deeper into our past and the different narratives we tell ourselves and others, whether they be positive or negative, as well as why we tell them, later in this chapter. But first we'd like to share how and why research into dying and grieving came about in the United States and other Western cultures.

The Genesis of Dying and Grief Research

We have Elisabeth Kübler-Ross to thank for taking on a topic Western society had basically ignored until she commenced researching it in the mid–1960s: how terminally ill people are affected by the knowledge that they are going to die and, ultimately, how it affects those left behind.

Her groundbreaking work began when, as a faculty member at the University of Colorado School of Medicine, she was asked by a colleague to lecture medical students on any topic. Kübler-Ross had been born and raised in Switzerland but had lived in the United States for a few years. In that time, she had noticed that American doctors seemed nervous around terminally ill patients and wondered how they should approach death and dying. She conducted a two-part lecture. In the first part, she examined how different cultures approach death. In the second part, she asked a sixteen-year-old girl dying of leukemia to answer questions and speak to the audience. Kübler-Ross noted the medical students were riveted and, like the doctors she'd previously observed, nervous. Rather than delving into the girl's thoughts and feelings about her impending death, they asked only clinical questions about her physical symptoms.

This lecture further piqued Kübler-Ross's interest, and for the next five years, she interviewed the terminally ill, studied their needs, and conducted seminars on her findings. But some of her colleagues found her conferences ruthless, as patients were asked to confront their deaths. In those days—and, in some realms, even now—the accepted belief was that patients don't want or need to know whether they are terminally ill. In addition, some doctors didn't want to openly admit that a patient might be dying. The truth was often shared only with family members, and, when broached with the patient, it was spoken roundaboutly with euphemisms. Kübler-Ross felt these beliefs and practices were antiquated, if not cowardly, and that medical professionals owed their patients the truth.

• • •

Throughout this book, we'll share our personal experiences of losing loved ones and the grief that caught and tumbled us in the wake of their deaths. These vignettes are placed in particular sections to emphasize the topic. We'll start with Rick, Rose's husband, and his stage 3 gastric cancer.

Rick and Rose: How We Found Out Rick Was Dying

Eleven months after the diagnosis, Rick's new primary care physician asked us to come in for a visit following his review of the most recent results from Rick's oncology report. We had met this doctor only once before and had been told he was deeply religious. Although we were unfamiliar with his mannerisms, the serious look on his face spoke volumes. He asked how Rick was doing but seemed distracted when Rick answered that he thought he was doing well. The doctor nodded and then launched into a short speech about politics, the state of our nation, and taxes, which was odd. When he was done, he didn't come right out and tell us Rick had turned the final corner on the path of hopeful optimism and was now heading toward the dead-end fact that there was nothing more to be done or that Rick was dying. Instead, he shot me a meaningful glance and then looked Rick in the eye and said, "We should all be right with the Big Guy upstairs, all the time," followed by "Nothing is certain in this life except death and taxes." It was then that I realized how he was trying to tie in the earlier part of his speech with Rick's imminent demise.

He stepped out to give Rick and me a couple of minutes to ponder what had just happened. Rick was confused, still in denial about the seriousness of his fatal disease. Trying to make sense of what he had just been told, he asked me what I thought the doctor meant. Was he suggesting Rick start going to church? Maybe that we should get a new CPA to do our taxes? I hugged Rick close and said we'd talk on the way home. Then the doctor returned and asked to see me in the hallway, alone. I smiled at Rick, who looked bewildered, and said I'd be back in a sec.

(This experience transitions into another topic and is continued in Chapter Three, under "Rick and Rose: Everything Everywhere All at Once.")

• • •

In 1969, Kübler-Ross's book *On Death and Dying* was released, and an article about her work and one of her seminars was published in *Life* magazine. Although grateful readers thanked her for starting the conversation about death, administrators at the hospital where she worked were furious about the article as well as the focus of her book. As a result, her contract was not renewed. Fortunately, her book became a bestseller and she was soon lecturing nationwide at universities and hospitals.

Kübler-Ross proposed that patients frequently knew they were dying and wanted their situation to be acknowledged, not disregarded: "The patient is in the process of losing everything and everybody he loves. If he is allowed to express his sorrow he will find a final acceptance much easier." Further, she posited that dying people experienced five stages on their final journey: denial, anger, bargaining, depression, and acceptance. In the following decades, Kübler-Ross suggested that family members and loved ones also experienced these stages, which culminated in another book, coauthored with David Kessler, *On Grief and Grieving* (first released in 2005).

Kübler-Ross's Five Stages of Grief

We've noted in our work in grief counseling, as well as through personal experience, that there is no specific length of time for each stage of grief, nor do they consistently follow the order presented below. As a mourner, you may experience one for a few minutes or hours, then another for a day or more, and then *bam!*, you're back to the previous stage or have jumped ahead to another. It's also possible to experience more than one stage at a time as well as have lengthy periods when you feel okay, only to be drawn back into grief by a trigger or thought. Just remember: It's all normal.

Also, we've noted that not everyone experiences all of these stages— for example, you may not experience the anger or bargaining stages of grief. We hypothesize that this may be due to personality, beliefs, and/or situational circumstances.

Denial is the first stage, in which we are overwhelmed, in a state of shock, and in denial. How could this be happening? How can we carry on? We try to work through the numbness and get through each day. Shock and denial are natural. It's our brain helping us cope with an impossible situation, allowing us to pace our grief. Otherwise, the information and emotions we might feel all at once would be too much to handle. When we begin to accept reality—that we will suffer (or have already suffered) a loss—we begin to heal, we become stronger, and this stage begins to fade. Then the feelings we denied start to surface.

Anger is part of the healing process, and the more we feel it, the more it will dissipate. Anger may mask other emotions that will eventually emerge. For many, it's generally the easiest emotion to manage, as most have learned to tamp anger down since it's feared and frowned on by society. During this stage, we may feel anger toward loved ones, friends, doctors, the person who is dying (or has died), and, if you are a believer, even God. Behind the anger are our feelings of pain. But anger can strengthen us during this time of loss. Many people have been taught by culture or society to suppress their anger rather than feel, express and process it. However, anger can be an indication of how intense our love is for the one who passed.

Bargaining, when it occurs during terminal illness, may take the form of making promises to do anything to get better or help our ill loved one. When bargaining occurs after a loss, it may present as a tradeoff—for instance, good deeds—in the hope that our loved one will miraculously be restored. "If only…" or "What if…" are common trains of thoughts during this stage. The root of the bargaining stage is our feeling of helplessness. Thus, we live in the past, negotiating with the present and masking the pain we feel while wishing things would go back to normal. Feelings of guilt are often bargaining's twin, as we are stuck in our own personal *Groundhog Day*, finding fault in our previous actions and re-creating what might have been if only we'd done this one thing differently.

Depression is the stage after bargaining, when reality hits and we realize we're in the present. This type of depression is actually *situational depression*, as a particular situation is causing the depression. At this time, grief sets in on a deeper, more intense level. Depression during grief is appropriate and common, not a sign of mental illness. During this stage, isolation and withdrawal from the life we'd known before our loss is normal. It may feel like we're in a dense fog of profound sorrow and that it may never go away. But losing a loved one *is* depressing; in fact, it would be highly unusual if a person *wasn't* depressed after losing a loved one. Others, especially those who have not experienced what you have endured (or who are from a culture or ascribe to a belief system in which depression is a sign of weakness), either don't understand or are wrong thinking. You can't just flip a switch and turn it off. You have to feel it in order to heal.

Acceptance is the last stage of grief, when we accept the loss of our loved one and our new reality. Acceptance does not mean we are okay with our loss, for we are forever changed and life is very different now. But we can learn to live without our loved one as we move forward into a new and different future. Some may try to carry on with their lives as they did before their loved one died, as if the loss didn't happen. But over time, acceptance in one of its many forms (perhaps by cleaning a closet or chest of drawers) creeps in and the façade begins to crumble. Family roles may change, and relationships may strengthen—or even dissolve—as we learn to organize our day-to-day lives. In time, we'll have more good days than bad, and although it may seem impossible, we'll learn to enjoy life again.

New Research

In the years since Kübler-Ross's book on grief was published, new research has revealed that grief is an ongoing process that may or may not end. In the past, most mental health professionals believed that the bereaved needed to let go of their loved one or the loss in order to move forward. But studies in other nations, such as China, where the bereaved continue a relationship with their dead ancestors, indicate that they suffer less long-term distress than mourning Americans do.

Further, scientists have determined that, like fear, grief is a reaction to stress that can cause deep physiological changes. Just as stress can weaken an immune system, disturb sleep, and increase stress hormones such as cortisol, so can grief. It's also not unusual for the bereaved to suffer from loss of appetite, heart palpitations caused by anxiety, and imaginings based on internalized beliefs, such as believing their loved one appears to them, perhaps in the form of a butterfly or bird.

The stages of grief are a tool for those in mourning. They help identify what we might be feeling during our bereavement. But, as mentioned previously, grief and its stages aren't set in concrete. Grief is fluid and doesn't know linear time. For all of us, grief is an individual experience with a narrative that is as singular as each individual.

Time perspective therapy understands the unique time perspective narrative we tell ourselves based on our personal experiences. This perspective is the lens through which we view our lives. When we are mourning, the idea of having a forward-leaning new framework, a more hope-filled narrative, can be a welcome ray of light that permanently illuminates the darkness in our lives.

This is the first of three vignettes by Phil about his life experiences with loss and grief.

Phil: Dead Children in My Hospital Were "Going Home"

When I was five years old, I spent five months in a hospital in New York City for children with contagious diseases; I had whooping cough and double pneumonia. The year was 1938, long before penicillin and sulfa drugs were available to treat such illnesses. That meant I simply spent all the time in my bed, never exercising or walking. I made up mental games that I shared with the children in beds near mine. However, quite often when I awoke and my friend in the nearby bed was not there, the nurse told me that he had gone home. When I asked her why he did not say goodbye, she said he left in the middle of the night and did not want to bother me. After several repetitions, I became suspicious that "going home" meant that the child had died! It was a terrible experience because what I wanted most was to "go home," but not to "go home" in that bad way, but rather in the good way—to be with my family again in our little apartment. One day, the head nurse came to my bedside and told me that the time had come for me to "go home." She did not understand when I started to cry and then reassured me that my parents were waiting downstairs to take me back to where I had come from five months earlier. It was the happiest moment in my young life!

Bias Toward the Past

Everyone experiences good and bad things, but not everyone sees the world in the same way or attaches the same importance to these experiences. In other words, some of us instinctively look toward the brighter side of life (past positive) while others tend to focus on the shadows and the dark (past negative). We have found, for the most part, that people who focus on the past value the old more than the new; the familiar over the novel; and the cautious, conservative approach over the daring, more risky one. How we view the past—positively or negatively—informs the narratives we tell ourselves and others.

When a person has a *past positive* point of view, they are constantly reminded of the good experiences in their past. It's easy for them to remember an abundance of wonderful things that happened throughout their life. This perspective may cause them to judge, evaluate and react to everything in the present moment through memories of these happy past experiences. Overall, people who have a past positive viewpoint tend to be less anxious than those with a past negative perspective. They also tend to be happier, healthier, and more successful.

When a person has a *past negative* point of view, they judge, evaluate, and react to everything in the present moment through memories of unhappy past experiences. They live their lives under a dark cloud in which their regrets, failures and illnesses constantly surround them. When a tragedy or trauma occurs to them, unlike most people, who will process and move on with their lives, they can't let it go or move forward. Instead, they are stuck, facing backward as they replay what happened over and over again in their mind. (As an aside, people with post-traumatic stress or major depression usually have a high past negative score.)

People with a bias toward the past live in a world where everything new reminds them of something old. We're pretty sure someone you know—perhaps a relative at a family gathering, or even you!—has said, "Remember when…" or "This is just like that time we…" or "This reminds me of…" These are past-oriented remembrances. (As an aside, this also happens more frequently as we age and short-term memory dissipates. It may be the reason we sometimes hear the same story from someone we know or love over and over again.)

If you are usually an upbeat person but have experienced a traumatic loss, you may temporarily find yourself with a past negative time perspective. As the weeks and months progress, you'll more than likely slowly return to your original positive time perspective.

• • •

Religions and Spiritual Practices: How We Mourn—Part 2

Continuing our exploration of religions and grieving, we're devoting this section to the religion with the greatest population: Christianity. In the twenty-first century, there are an estimated 2.2 billion Christians worldwide. Until the Protestant Reformation swept through Europe in the 1500s, the Christian Church was largely composed of two groups (or denominations): the Roman Catholic Church in the west and the Greek Orthodox Church in the east. Through the years, numerous other denominations have been established, most in the last century or so, including Protestant, Eastern Orthodox, Anglican and Non-Trinitarian. For our purposes, we'll focus on Christianity overall as well as the two original denominations.

CHRISTIANITY

Interestingly, the influence of Queen Victoria, although mostly diminished, continues to be felt in some grieving practices. In nineteenth-century England, Queen Victoria mourned the death of her husband Prince Albert (who died of typhoid at age forty-two) for forty years and wore only black until the end of her life. Victoria was the head of the Church of England and a beloved monarch in a time when the mortality rate was high. The people of the Victorian era romanticized death and the melancholia of grief. Death was accepted, even fashionable, likely because it was inescapable for many, no matter their age or social class, due to widespread diseases like typhoid, cholera, smallpox, and scarlet fever. For the upper class, postmortem photography was a trend. There was a strict dress code for the grieving family, especially the widow, who wore only black for a period of at least one year. Jewelry featuring black stones and personal mementos, like a lock of hair, were popular accessories and expressions of grief.

Most modern Christian denominations have no strictly designated periods of mourning. Former guidelines are not as set as they were in the past, evolving and influenced by culture and convenience. The loss of such structure is arguably a contributing factor in today's changing views regarding how we experience grief, as well as the lack of solace once afforded by one's religion. However, certain Victorian era–inspired practices continue to this day, such as the wearing of black and the importance of personal mementos of the deceased. People in today's society are not as likely to seek the counsel of clergy as was once commonplace in predominantly Christian Western culture. However, most denominations offer the comfort of ritual and security of custom for their congregations, and many find peace through their houses of worship.

Eastern Orthodox Christians observe very specific memorial dates within a forty-day period. These memorials, which include special rites, prayers, and food preparations, are to take place at three, six, and nine months; one year; and the death anniversary for a period of at least seven years. Close family members may mourn for one year, during which time the widow/widower will wear only black.

The *Roman Catholic Church* officially distinguishes three types of mourning, the length of which is dependent on the relationship shared with the deceased. Heavy (or deep) mourning is the most intense period of grief, followed by half mourning, and concluding with light (or second) mourning. Moving through these phases is considered optional in today's church, but guidelines are afforded. In the heavy phase of grieving, all black dress is appropriate; in some cultures, all white clothing may also be acceptable. During half mourning, black with white trim or white with black trim is standard. During the final stages of light mourning, mild colors, soft pastels and prints are acceptable.

In today's world, mourning attire is often worn only at church and on formal occasions. The duration of these periods of mourning has been reassessed in modern times and may or may not be adhered to according to one's personal preference and level of commitment to church rituals. The modern Catholic Church sets guidelines of a "one year and a day" period of mourning for a spouse; the church also advises lesser periods of time spent on the three types of mourning for other family members who seek guidance on this matter.

• • •

Similarities Between Grief and Post-traumatic Stress

Time perspective therapy was originally developed to help people overcome post-traumatic stress disorder (PTSD or PTS). For those unfamiliar with this mental injury, it's well worth exploring, especially since grief and post-traumatic stress share symptoms. Post-traumatic stress can happen when a person is directly exposed to a traumatic event or witnesses a traumatic event happening to others. It can occur on learning that a traumatic experience involved a close family member or friend. It can also be the result of repeated exposure to horrible details of trauma, such as first responders or case workers exposed to details of child abuse cases.

In TPT, we refer to PTS as a mental "injury" instead of "disorder" or "illness" because of its similarity to a physical injury. It's as if one minute you're okay, and the next you're not. For example, imagine that one moment you're sitting on the branch of a tree, enjoying a magnificent sunset. You're content; everything is right with the world. Suddenly, you lose your balance, fall and break your arm. Depending on how bad the break is, you may need different types of treatment, but once it's taken care of properly, sooner or later, your broken arm will heal.

If you have a mild case of PTS—for example, you were in a fender bender, and while you suffered no serious injury, for a month or more you've had intrusive thoughts and dreams about the accident—there's a good chance you'll get better on your own over time. However, if you have moderate to severe PTS—perhaps the accident involved a more serious injury or even death—if at all possible, it's important to see a therapist to help you understand, cope with, and eventually overcome the trauma.

To drive this point home, if you broke your arm, you wouldn't put a bandage on it and think you're good to go. Over time, any number of horrible things could happen, like infection or gangrene (to say nothing of the pain you will experience); in the worst-case scenario, you could lose your arm. Instead, you'd go to the emergency room or see your physician as soon as possible. Your arm would be reset or, if necessary, you'd have surgery, and then you'd get a cast to protect and strengthen your injured arm. The same is true of moderate to severe PTS. You shouldn't ignore the symptoms (depression, angry outbursts, lack of concentration, sleep disturbances, to name a few) and think they'll go away, because over time, instead of going away, there is a chance they'll do the opposite—they'll increase. (For more information about acute anxiety and PTS, see the diagnostic criteria listed in the following section.)

For some people reading this book, the grief you feel for the loss of a loved one may be intensified if the cause of death was traumatic or if the experience was traumatic for you. We'd like to revisit how grief is similar to post-traumatic stress in that it can be deeply embedded in the brain. Just like post-traumatic stress, grief isn't located in any one part of the brain because our memories, as well as sight, smell, hearing, physical sensation or pain, are all stored in different areas. This means that sad or painful thoughts can be triggered whenever one of these senses reminds us of our loss.

Here are a few ways being reminded of our deceased loved one might send us into a spiral of bittersweet memories:

- Seeing their photo, or their favorite color, or a personal article
- Smelling something we associate with the deceased
- Preparing or eating their favorite food
- Hearing a particular song or melody that was special for the deceased

All of these things may bring us fleeting happiness followed by sadness—or just straight up sadness. And all of these experiences are similar to the effects of PTS. To be clear, it's not a bad thing to recall past negative experiences; we learn from them, and they have helped make us who we are today. But if we are stuck going over and over what happened in the past, and if these memories are holding us back from living a richer, fuller life, it's beneficial to learn a coping skill so we can move on.

• • •

Directly following a traumatic event, one may be diagnosed with acute anxiety if they have some or all of the symptoms listed below for up to a month. If the person's symptoms last for more than one month, they may have post-traumatic stress. What follows is the official American Psychiatric Association definition of the post-traumatic stress disorder diagnosis (please note that these criteria apply to adults, adolescents, and children older than six years; for younger children, see the DSM-5 section titled "Post-traumatic Stress Disorder for Children 6 Years and Younger").

Exhibit 1.3–4 DSM-5 Diagnostic Criteria for PTSD

A. Exposure to actual or threatened death, serious injury, or sexual violence in one (or more) of the following ways:
   1. Directly experiencing the traumatic event(s).
   2. Witnessing, in person, the event(s) as it occurred to others.
   3. Learning that the traumatic event(s) occurred to a close family member or close friend. In cases of actual or threatened death of a family member or friend, the event(s) must have been violent or accidental.
   4. Experiencing repeated or extreme exposure to aversive details of the traumatic event(s) (e.g., first responders collecting human remains; police officers repeatedly exposed to details of child abuse). Note: Criterion A4 does not apply to exposure through electronic media, television, movies, or pictures, unless this exposure is work related.

B. Presence of one (or more) of the following intrusion symptoms associated with the traumatic event(s), beginning after the traumatic event(s) occurred:
   1. Recurrent, involuntary, and intrusive distressing memories of the traumatic event(s). **Note:** In children older than 6 years, repetitive play may occur in which themes or aspects of the traumatic event(s) are expressed.
   2. Recurrent distressing dreams in which the content and/or affect of the dream are related to the traumatic event(s). **Note:** In children, there may be frightening dreams without recognizable content.
   3. Dissociative reactions (e.g., flashbacks) in which the individual feels or acts as if the traumatic event(s) were recurring. (Such reactions may occur on a continuum, with the most extreme expression being a complete loss of awareness of present surroundings.) **Note:** In children, trauma-specific reenactment may occur in play.
   4. Intense or prolonged psychological distress at exposure to internal or external cues that symbolize or resemble an aspect of the traumatic event(s).

5. Marked physiological reactions to internal or external cues that symbolize or resemble an aspect of the traumatic event(s).

C. Persistent avoidance of stimuli associated with the traumatic event(s), beginning after the traumatic event(s) occurred, as evidenced by one or both of the following:
    1. Avoidance of or efforts to avoid distressing memories, thoughts, or feelings about or closely associated with the traumatic event(s).
    2. Avoidance of or efforts to avoid external reminders (people, places, conversations, activities, objects, situations) that arouse distressing memories, thoughts, or feelings about or closely associated with the traumatic event(s).

D. Negative alterations in cognitions and mood associated with the traumatic event(s), beginning or worsening after the traumatic event(s) occurred, as evidenced by two (or more) of the following:
    1. Inability to remember an important aspect of the traumatic event(s) (typically due to dissociative amnesia, and not to other factors such as head injury, alcohol, or drugs).
    2. Persistent and exaggerated negative beliefs or expectations about oneself, others, or the world (e.g., "I am bad," "No one can be trusted," "The world is completely dangerous," "My whole nervous system is permanently ruined").
    3. Persistent, distorted cognitions about the cause or consequences of the traumatic event(s) that lead the individual to blame himself/herself or others.
    4. Persistent negative emotional state (e.g., fear, horror, anger, guilt, or shame).
    5. Markedly diminished interest or participation in significant activities.
    6. Feelings of detachment or estrangement from others.
    7. Persistent inability to experience positive emotions (e.g., inability to experience happiness, satisfaction, or loving feelings).

E. Marked alterations in arousal and reactivity associated with the traumatic event(s), beginning or worsening after the traumatic event(s) occurred, as evidenced by two (or more) of the following:
    1. Irritable behavior and angry outbursts (with little or no provocation), typically expressed as verbal or physical aggression toward people or objects.
    2. Reckless or self-destructive behavior.
    3. Hypervigilance.
    4. Exaggerated startle response.
    5. Problems with concentration.
    6. Sleep disturbance (e.g., difficulty falling or staying asleep or restless sleep).

F. Duration of the disturbance (Criteria B, C, D and E) is more than 1 month.
G. The disturbance causes clinically significant distress or impairment in social, occupational, or other important areas of functioning.
H. The disturbance is not attributable to the physiological effects of a substance (e.g., medication, alcohol) or another medical condition.

Specify whether:

With dissociative symptoms: The individual's symptoms meet the criteria for post-traumatic stress disorder, and in addition, in response to the stressor, the individual experiences persistent or recurrent symptoms of either of the following:

1. **Depersonalization:** Persistent or recurrent experiences of feeling detached from, and as if one were an outside observer of, one's mental processes or body (e.g., feeling as though one were in a dream; feeling a sense of unreality of self or body or of time moving slowly).
2. **Derealization:** Persistent or recurrent experiences of unreality of surroundings (e.g., the world around the individual is experienced as unreal, dreamlike, distant, or distorted). **Note:** To use this subtype, the dissociative symptoms must not be attributable to the physiological effects of a substance (e.g., blackouts, behavior during alcohol intoxication) or another medical condition (e.g., complex partial seizures).

Specify whether:

With delayed expression: If the full diagnostic criteria are not met until at least 6 months after the event (although the onset and expression of some symptoms may be immediate).

https://www.ncbi.nlm.nih.gov/books/NBK207191/box/part1_ch3.box16/

Phil: The Boy Scout Home Funeral

When I was twelve years old, I had just started my first term in the local Boy Scout troop. At this time, one of my friends had died suddenly of some disease. We were all invited to come to his home to say farewell to our little buddy. The room was darkened, lit only by some candles on either side of his coffin. We were instructed to go one by one to hold his hand while we said a farewell prayer to him. As I was doing so, I fainted, as did several other Scouts. We were each taken to the kitchen and given some orange juice to help refresh us. However, none of us wanted to go back into that room, where a priest was leading a farewell prayer. I felt guilty for being such a frail Scout, especially when recalling that our motto was to always be brave and strong.

Changing Past Negatives into Past Positives

Grief can be all consuming; it can wash over us like a tsunami and, on occasion, carry us away in waves. Sometimes we barely have a chance to catch our breath before we're caught in another wave of sadness and despair. But grief doesn't have to control our lives. We can choose to be proactive and change our thought patterns when appropriate. For instance, when we're stuck in grief for an extended length of time—which is past negative—by drawing on past positive memories, we begin to reclaim our lives in the present and clear the way for our new future. As stated earlier, it's not a bad thing to have past negative thoughts—we just don't want to get stuck inside them. The more we practice replacing past negative thoughts with happy recollections, the easier it becomes and, eventually, the better and more in control we will feel.

Now that we have a greater understanding of the different aspects of grief and how grief might affect us, we're ready to begin our personal time perspective journey. We'll stretch and flex our new mental muscles and learn new skills, including a simple breathing technique to use prior to doing our mind exercises. You can use the breathing method whenever you start to feel anxious or want to unwind and relax.

Knowing how grief affects you personally is the first step to overcoming any symptoms you may be experiencing. When we are grieving, we may have a hard time thinking about anything other than our loss and how it's changed our life. We're stuck here in the present, facing the wrong way, toward the past. There's little or no room for thoughts of the present or the future. Let's change that. But first, there's someone we'd like you to meet.

• • •

We searched for a study that determined how many people seek grief therapy after they lose a loved one. Unfortunately, we were unable to find such research. That's not to say it doesn't exist; it's just that we may not have access to this type of information at this time—or that it's a near impossible task to accomplish. What we do know is that around 2.5 million people die in the United States annually, each leaving an average of five grieving people behind. And it's estimated that 1.5 million children (5 percent of the children in the United States) have lost one or both of their parents by age fifteen.

We can presume with a fair amount of confidence that most people who have lost a loved one do *not* seek grief therapy. And the majority of our population hasn't been to (or will ever need to be in) therapy. But it may be helpful for you to see how time perspective grief therapy sessions look and feel. This is not to suggest that if you are grieving, you need to see a therapist (or a time perspective therapist in particular). We hope we've provided enough information in this book so that you can do this therapy on your own. But should you realize you need some extra help, please do seek it. And if the therapist you choose is unfamiliar with TPT, maybe share this book with them.

At this time, we'd like to introduce you to Noelle, a former client. We have changed Noelle's name, as well as the names of her husband and adult child, to protect their privacy. She graciously gave us permission to share her history and wanted people who have lost a loved one to know that if she was able to overcome her deep grief, it is possible for others to do so as well. Throughout Chapters Two, Three, and Four, we'll tell her story and also share some of her therapist's notes.

Noelle

When Noelle sought grief counseling, she was a beautiful fifty-year-old woman. Brought up in a Catholic family, Noelle had attended parochial school. While in high school, she had a secret crush on Brian, a popular, handsome young man two years older than her. To Noelle's great surprise, when she was a senior in high school, Brian asked her out, thus commencing a three-year courtship. After high school, Noelle attended business college for two years in another town. She returned home as frequently as she could to be with her family and see Brian, usually once or twice a month. They were married shortly after she graduated from college.

Noelle and Brian couldn't have been more different. She was shy and reserved; he was outgoing and high spirited. Brian, being a charismatic person, had numerous friends—some since childhood, others from college and work. These friends, along with their spouses, became friends with Noelle. Noelle worked as an accountant for a large corporation. Brian was a firefighter. As the years progressed, he climbed the administrative ladder in the fire department. They had two energetic, sports-minded children, a boy and a girl. For nearly thirty years, they were devoted to each other, their family, and their church. Brian eventually retired and established a business on their family farm with their now adult children. Noelle continued to work for the same corporation she had since graduating from college. She also handled the accounting for the family business.

Unfortunately, during the holidays, Brian fell ill. He died unexpectedly of a ruptured appendix. Let's hear from Noelle in her own words what happened:

Brian was a firefighter and had a background in emergency medical care. He worked twenty-four hours on and twenty-four hours off for four shifts and then had several days off in a row. This was a good schedule for him because we have a farm, so, with the help of our kids, he was able to run the farm and care for the animals. He never went to the doctor when he was sick. If he needed stitches, he'd sew them himself! When he asked me to take him to the clinic, I knew he must have had a really bad flu. It was during the holidays, so there were very few people working. We had to wait five hours, and Brian kept getting weaker. When we finally saw the doctor, he said Brian had the stomach flu and sent us home. But the whole drive home, the light was going out of Brian's eyes. It was four in the afternoon and the sun was out, but he said it was dark.

When we got home, our children helped Brian into our bedroom. I was confused and numb from what was happening. I kept thinking, "The doctor sent me home with a dying man." My kids wanted me out of the bedroom because they were concerned for me. When I was leaving the room, I glanced at Brian. He was very weak, but he motioned for me to come to him. By this time, he couldn't talk, but he gestured for me to come closer. I thought he wanted to tell me something. He looked deeply in my eyes—his eyes so full of love—and I put my ear near his mouth. He leaned in and kissed me on the cheek.... I knew he was trying to convey something to me. I just didn't know it was a goodbye.

The ambulance came and Brian was taken to the hospital. He died a few hours later of a ruptured appendix.

You never think that the one and only man you've slept beside for twenty-eight years won't be there anymore ... that he might be taken before his time ... that he won't be here to kiss and touch and love. You never think that there will be no more family holidays together ... that the grandchildren yet to come will never know how wonderful their grandpa was.... I was devastated. How could I handle everything Brian did? I couldn't think about it.

A couple of weeks after Brian died, I returned to work. I knew I wasn't ready, but I was afraid I'd lose my job. I thought I was handling everything well, but I started having severe chest pains. After a series of tests, my doctor said my heart was fine and that I was having panic attacks. He referred me to a psychiatrist[1] who prescribed antianxiety and antidepression medications. I took them but didn't think they helped much. I had such a hard time whenever I had an appointment because they were at the same clinic where the doctor had misdiagnosed Brian. Every time I went there, I would have flashbacks to Brian's death and wonder how they could have sent me home with a dying husband.

About five months after Brian died, I saw a friend, and she told me that this therapist had helped her daughter, who lost her young husband in a car accident. I had been going to the clinic for help, but I thought it was a good idea to see someone outside.

The first time I saw the time perspective therapist, I cried and cried. I told her what happened to Brian and how I wasn't myself anymore—I felt like I was half a person. She explained the stages of grief (denial, anger, bargaining, depression and acceptance) and said that, along with being in the denial stage of grief, I probably had PTS because I was there when my husband died. She told me about TPT and asked me to watch a relaxation video that had a breathing technique that would help calm me. I was supposed to practice this breathing technique every day. I took some psychological tests, and we set up sessions once a week.

In the next session, I admitted I didn't watch the video. I wanted to talk about Brian and the clinic and what happened at the hospital. I wasn't ready to stop grieving.

In the following sessions, I told the TP therapist I wasn't able to do a good job at work because I was having flashbacks and my mind would race. She helped me understand my PTS symptoms. I still hadn't done the breathing exercise. I couldn't sleep at night. I missed my husband.

I had left all of Brian's things exactly as he left them. His watch was on the nightstand. His toiletries were in the bathroom. The shoes he took off before he came into the house the last time were still near the mudroom doorway. Many months had gone by, but I hadn't moved or put away any of his things. Part of me was still waiting for him to come home from work.

I was still in denial. I wanted to think I was doing better than I really was, so I cut back my therapy sessions to twice a month. But I was becoming

---

1. The difference between a psychiatrist and a psychologist: A psychiatrist is a medical doctor who can diagnose and prescribe medication to treat mental health disorders. Psychiatrists treat from the point of view that there is a chemical imbalance in the brain that medication can help correct. A psychologist or therapist, by contrast, uses talk therapy to help treat mental health symptoms and trauma and to improve how stress and relationships are managed.

obsessed with finding answers to why Brian had died. I went to church services—not just my faith, but every faith I could find. I was very, very angry—not at the doctor who misdiagnosed Brian. He was just trying to finish up the day and get home to his family. I was rageful toward the clinic for being understaffed. And I realized I was mad at Brian for leaving me.

Throughout the sessions, the TP therapist listened. She tried to get me to focus on the positive things that had happened in my life before Brian's death, but I couldn't really go there. It was too painful. She suggested I do simple, fun things with my children, but I didn't think I deserved to have fun. My husband was dead; my life was over. I was afraid. I couldn't think about the future without Brian. But I would try, and those times I did go out with my children, I forgot my sorrow for a while. But it always came back because I would think about Brian. I was having a good time without him.

The TP therapist was concerned about my kids, and in every session she would ask how they were doing. My son was a lot like his father and thought he should handle things on his own. He didn't think he needed therapy, so he never went. My daughter, Lily, wanted some help, so she started therapy. She met with the TP therapist four times. I don't know what happened in those sessions, but Lily seemed so much more confident and had a way of calming me. I found out later that she was learning ways to help me and the rest of the family.

I stopped eating. Food didn't taste like anything. I would visit Brian's grave and talk to him. He would talk to me too. I felt so sorrowful. It felt like he was trying to pull me into the grave with him. It got so bad that one day I checked myself into the psych ward at the hospital. I stayed for four days.

You know, the people in the psych ward were just like you or me. They weren't crazy; they were just having a hard time with life. We met in a group every day, and my psychiatrist visited me. He told me I had become "situationally psychotic"—that this wasn't normal for me. But because of Brian's death, I went overboard. He was a little miffed with me because I had cut back my therapy sessions. Then he increased my medications and told me I had to see my therapist every week. I hadn't even told her that I was in the hospital. But my psychiatrist called her and told her what had happened.

In my first session after returning from the hospital, the TP therapist explained how we can have subconscious thoughts of suicide. My faith wouldn't allow me to kill myself, but by not eating, and thinking that Brian was trying to pull me into the grave with him, I showed that I didn't want to live.

It had been many months since Brian had died, and he wouldn't want me to be sad or give up on life. She asked me to talk about all the good things—the past positives—in my life before Brian died. When I recalled them, I used as many of my senses as possible so they'd be easier to remember. She told me that all these good things were still inside me and that all the trauma and heartache I had experienced since Brian's death made me a stronger woman. She knew that I believe I'll see Brian again one day and we could continue to have a different sort of relationship. She also said at my age, I was very rich in experience. I listened and believed.

Whenever I had flashbacks or started to have negative thoughts, I replaced them with one of the positive memories I had of life with Brian. I did this so often, it became a habit.

Now we'll peer into Noelle's sessions through the eyes of her TP therapist.

Noelle's Journey from Past Negative to Past Positive

Noelle's primary care physician suggested she see a psychiatrist when the chest pains she was experiencing were determined to be caused by panic attacks. Her psychiatrist prescribed medications, which Noelle did not feel were helping her much. She had flashbacks to the time when her husband was dying whenever she had to go to the clinic to see her psychiatrist or attend other appointments. Consequently, she welcomed the idea of seeing a private therapist. She mentioned that she would rather pay out of pocket than have to go to the clinic every two weeks to see her psychiatrist.

In the course of the first TPT session, the therapist explained the basics of grief, PTS, and time perspective therapy. Noelle watched a relaxation video "The River of Time," (*https://www.youtube.com/watch?v=r4ZX0XVAa2A&t=256s*) that included a calming breathing technique (see "Take a Breath" later in this chapter) and was asked to watch it every day—mostly to practice the breathing method. During her first two months of treatment, Noelle was steeped in grief and PTS symptoms caused by witnessing her husband's death. She did not comply with either her psychiatrist's or her therapist's suggestions. She admitted to not practicing the breathing technique and became increasingly obsessive-compulsive, attending every religious service available to her and ceaselessly praying. Her ZTPI revealed high past negative, low past positive, high present fatalism, extremely low present hedonism, and moderately low future scores.

Although Noelle continued to work, her performance suffered due to PTS and grief symptoms such as racing thoughts and lack of concentration. She also harbored intense anger at the clinic and, she discovered, at her husband for leaving her. She continued to suffer severe flashbacks to her husband's death whenever she went to the clinic. At the zenith of her despair, she checked herself into the psychiatric ward at the hospital.

Meanwhile, one of Noelle's adult children, Lily, commenced TPT. She shared an insightful perspective of her mother's grief and PTS and how the rest of the family was doing. Lily had an excellent background in psychology and was interested in learning new ways to cope with the grief, stress, and anxiety that blanketed her family. She quickly grasped TPT and immediately began implementing what she had learned. During her four sessions, Lily was given tools shared in this book to help herself, her mother, and other family members. She felt she was equipped to handle future situations should they arise.

At the hospital, Noelle underwent group and individual therapy. While there, her psychiatrist increased her antidepressant and antianxiety medications. Four days later, she checked herself out and continued treatment with her psychiatrist, who recommended that she also resume weekly TPT sessions.

During her first therapy session following hospitalization, Noelle described how she had become psychotic and, when she visited her husband's gravesite, she felt he was pulling her into the grave with him. She was also hearing voices. Her loss of appetite for nourishment as well as life indicated subconscious forms of suicide.

The TP therapist explained to Noelle that she suffered from a mental injury, not a mental illness, caused by the terrible and unnecessary death of her beloved husband. Together they reviewed many of Noelle's past positive experiences. Noelle was asked to recall them each in as much detail as possible. While reviewing these memories, she realized that before Brian's death she had lived a happy life and enjoyed a deep spiritual connection with her husband and adult children.

The TP therapist mentioned that the youthful, vibrant woman Noelle had once been still existed within her, and experiencing the heartbreak she had recently endured added to her already rich life. Further, it would strengthen her and increase the depth of her character.

They practiced a simple breathing method that Noelle was encouraged to use daily and whenever she started to feel anxious or needed a few minutes of calm. Also, each day, whenever she noticed that past negative thoughts were weighing her down, she was to replace them immediately with one of the scores of past positive memories on which she could draw.

To be continued in Chapter Three: "The Present."

Let's Get Started

If you haven't taken the short-form ZTPI in Chapter One and plotted your scores on the graph in Appendix I, please do so before you start this section. It's important to know whether your past time perspective is past positive or past negative and whether your numerical score is high or low on the graph compared to the ideal. If your past negative and past positive scores are close to the ideal, then you're doing well. And although you might be tempted to skip ahead to Chapter Three, we encourage you to review the rest of this chapter, as it includes stress-reducing tips and other suggestions that may come in handy now or down the road.

If your *past negative score is above 3.0* and/or your *past positive score is below 3.22*, then at this time in your life you are leaning toward a past negative mindset, and we ask that you please proceed with this section.

• • •

We all have past positive memories, even if they're hard to remember when we're grieving. But they are there, just beneath the surface of our conscious thoughts. When we remember them and build a supply of past positive memories, in as much detail as possible, we're focusing on something other than our grief. Then, when we realize that we're slipping back into unwanted, past negative thoughts, we have a treasure trove of good memories we can draw on that will help us when we feel pulled too far or too deep into sorrow. This understanding allows us to stop facing back toward the past and turn around here in the present to face forward, looking toward our brighter and best future.

Building Your Treasure Chest
of Past Positive Memories

When someone to whom we are close has died (especially if we witnessed it), different parts of the brain can be triggered whenever we see, hear or experience something that reminds us of our loss. And frequently we don't handle things as well as we used to. Perhaps now we're

58

short tempered or irritated by things that didn't bother us before, or lack of sleep or nourishment causes us to overreact to people and situations that we would have easily handled in the past. Or the opposite may occur: we may not even bother reacting to situations to which we should react or responding to people we know and love. Sometimes we may not recognize this new person we've become—or the person we used to be.

Overcoming grief starts with a choice: we can choose to be stuck in what happened, or we can accept that life is different now and move forward with our lives. Being mindful of our thoughts (especially the negative thoughts that are holding us back from doing what we want or need to do) is the first step on our path to well-being. Then we can start moving forward by replacing sad thoughts of our past with positive memories. In time, and with practice, we'll be well on our way to living a more hopeful life. After all, we can't change what happened, but we can come to a kind of peace through acceptance. Our loss may have changed the way we think or the way we view ourselves and the world. And now it is part of our past, part of our life experience, part of who we are.

• • •

Start by finding a comfortable position in a place where you feel safe and won't be interrupted. You could be seated on a cozy chair or sofa in a quiet room, sitting cross legged on the floor, or lying on a bed or yoga mat. Wherever you are, we hope it is a place where you can relax and allow yourself five uninterrupted minutes.

Take a Breath

Before going further, it is essential to clear our thoughts to aid our search for good memories. Our goal is to refocus from the constant chatter in our mind to the life-sustaining breaths we frequently take for granted. By doing this, we'll help clear the way for past positive memories to come to us. The best way to achieve this result is to take a few moments to *breathe*.

If there is another breathing technique that you are familiar with, feel free to use it instead of the one we'll suggest. Or, if after you've tried this method a few times you find it helpful to breathe even slower and add more numbers to your breaths—for instance, some people prefer to inhale and exhale to a count of seven instead of four—then please do so. The number of breaths you take is also flexible. Additional breaths beyond the four suggested in this technique can be included if you're having a difficult time relaxing.

This is the breathing technique we use before we begin our TPT exercises. You are welcome to use this method at any time of day or night, whenever you start to feel anxious, need to focus on a task, or collect your thoughts.

- Close your eyes. Clear your mind by focusing on your breathing. Breathe slowly, fully, deeply, and rhythmically. Allow your body to relax deeper and deeper with each breath. Feel the day's tension melting away.
- Inhale to a slow count of four.
- Pause for a moment, holding your breath.
- Now exhale to a slow count of four.
- Pause for a moment before continuing.
- Repeat three more times.

Good Memories

Once you've completed four (or more) of these relaxing breaths, you're ready to gently shift focus to a past positive memory that makes you feel good. Depending on the level of your depression or grief, you may not be able to think of anything that makes you feel good or positive right now, much less try to remember a positive experience from the past. So, take your time. And if you're having difficulty during this process, you can always return focus to your breathing.

Now, imagine going back in time to the first good memory that comes to mind. This memory may be from earlier in the day, or yesterday, last week, last year, or as far back as your childhood. This past positive experience may or may not include the loved one who passed. Some people find it helpful to visualize; if this is the case for you, then imagine you're looking into a pond of clear water and the happy memory is just under the surface. You can see. It's getting clearer. You remember. Now, recall this experience in as much detail as possible.

- What do you remember seeing around you at the time?
- Where were you?
- Were there any scents in the air?
- Who were you with?
- What were you doing?

Now recall two or more good memories, using as many of your five senses as possible. By doing this, you'll make the memories stronger and easier to access.

If, no matter how hard you try, you still can't recall a good or happy memory, then try to imagine what a past positive experience might have looked like. Doing that will likely lead you to remember an actual past positive followed by additional positive memories.

You may find this exercise difficult to complete at first, especially if you have undergone trauma. And it may not happen in your first attempt. But we've found that once you've remembered one good memory, the next one is usually easier to recall. By recalling several past positive memories in as much detail as possible, they'll come to you more swiftly when you need them. These positive memories are vital in modifying a past negative time perspective mindset.

Once you have a few past positive memories in your treasure chest, promise yourself that whenever you notice a past negative thought bringing you down, you will replace it immediately with one or more of your past positive memories. Sounds simple, but it works! The more you practice this technique, the easier it becomes.

So, each day, save some time—ideally five minutes, but even two or three minutes will do—to take a few breaths and recall a good memory. You're creating something precious: a treasure chest that will eventually be full of past positive memories that can sustain you during tough times.

A Good Night's Sleep

For many grieving people, nighttime (and particularly bedtime) is the most troublesome part of the day. Little by little, unsettling feelings can creep in as late afternoon fades into dusk and dusk melts into evening and then night. Without daily activities to keep our minds occupied and our bodies busy, as well as the unwanted pressure of knowing we're supposed to slow down, sadness and bothersome thoughts can overwhelm us. Grief is exhausting. And yet these feelings can make it difficult to relax and fall asleep. In many cases, the normal sleep pattern from before our loss is disrupted and can cause insomnia due to racing thoughts. Not knowing what else to do, we may find ourselves trying to relax by getting lost in screen time. But lights from electronics—television, computers, phones, and tablets—aren't helpful. In fact, they hamper our ability to sleep.

So, in order to unwind, it's important to allow some time—and some space—between your daily activities and bedtime. It can also be helpful to focus on relaxing your body and quieting your mind, especially if you're worried or anxious.

We've included two ways for you to relax your mind and body and prepare for sleep. We suggest you start by using the breathing technique described in the previous section. Doing so will help reset your mind and prepare you for what's next. Then try the following exercises, one after the other. Maybe you can try them tonight.

Walk away from work and your to-do list at least *one hour before* the start of your bedtime routine. Turn off your electronic devices *thirty minutes before* bedtime. If you take notes on your phone or tablet, rather than with pen and paper, then do the following reflection exercise before you turn off your electronic devices (thirty minutes before you go to bed). If, for whatever reason, this first exercise doesn't work for you, skip to the second. And maybe try the exercise again another night.

REFLECTION

After breathing slowly and deeply four or more times, take a few minutes of this quiet time to reflect on your day: Was there a high point? Were you able to do something you have been meaning to do (for instance, the dishes or the laundry, taking the dog for a walk, or grocery shopping)? Did you connect or communicate with anyone, whether in person, on the phone, or via messaging or Zoom? Can you remember seeing, hearing, or smelling something that brought you joy? When you reflect on the day, you'll very likely realize that even though what you did may appear small or insignificant, you *did* accomplish things and can feel good about these positive steps forward.

If you like, make a short list of what you accomplished today. Seeing your achievements in list form can give your self-esteem a little boost. Now, make a short list of the things you'd like to accomplish tomorrow. You're doing yourself a huge favor by putting these things—especially what you'd like to do in the future—on paper or in a note on your device because, for now, you can let them go. Now you won't have to stay awake thinking about them because they aren't taking up valuable space in your mind—space reserved for relaxation, healing, sleep and rejuvenation.

DEEP RELAXATION

As we learned in Chapter One, grief is a stressful experience. During this time, our bodies can be bombarded by an overwhelming amount of stress hormones. When our bodies are stressed, our muscles become tense. This muscle tension is like a reflex action—it's our body's way of guarding against what we may perceive to be injury or pain. This injury or pain doesn't necessarily have to be physical, because our bodies can also tense up if we feel our emotional health is threatened. This tension can happen for many reasons during the grieving process. We may feel stress and tense up whenever we think about our loss, or when someone with good intentions says something unhelpful, or if we *have* to do something with others when all we want to do is be alone.

Generally, with the sudden onset of stress, our muscles tighten up all at once and then release their tension when the stress passes. But if we're stressed for prolonged lengths of time, some of our muscles can end up in a constant state of guardedness. When this happens, other physical reactions may be triggered. For instance, migraine headaches and tension-type headaches can occur during the grieving process. These are associated with chronic muscle tension in the shoulders, neck and head. For this reason, we'll be spending a little more time on these areas.

This relaxation exercise, which focuses on your body and breath, can be used as a meditation technique at any time of the day or night. If you are using it for meditation, you do not need to be lying down. However, for our purposes now, we'll be using it as a sleep aid.

When you're lying in bed, get comfortable—whether in or out of your bedding is up to you. Ideally, you'll be lying on your back with your arms either at your sides or on your stomach or chest. Your legs can be straight or crossed at the ankles, or you can put a pillow under your knees if that feels good. Your head and neck should feel supported. If you can't lie on your back, then please assume whatever position is most comfortable for you. The goal here is to feel safe and cozy. These simple methods are tried and true. Trust in your own ability to make this process work for you, and be patient with yourself. You can do this.

Since stress is held in the muscles, you'll be focusing on each part of your body, gently flexing, maybe stretching, and relaxing your muscles. Throughout the day we don't often think about all the wonderful things our bodies do for us. This is a way to reconnect with our bodies before we sleep and allow our bodies to recuperate from the day's endeavors. During the second half of the exercise, when you exhale and relax the muscles in each part of your body, imagine the tension you've been holding there melting away. The repetitiveness of the exercise is intentional. It makes the exercise easier to remember and will ideally have a lulling effect.

We'll use the same breathing method mentioned previously, but you're welcome to use whatever technique you'd like. Begin by taking a slow, full, deep breath to the count of four. Hold it for a moment. Then slowly exhale to the count of four. Throughout the exercise, use this slow four-count breathing method whenever you inhale and exhale.

- Start with your *feet*. Flex and stretch your feet and toes as you breathe slowly, fully and deeply to a count of four. Hold your breath for a moment. Then slowly exhale to a count of four as you relax your feet and return them to where they were resting.
- Move to your *calves*. Flex your calf muscles as you breathe slowly, fully and deeply to a count of four. Hold for a moment. Then slowly exhale to a count of four as you relax your calves. (When doing your calves, it may be easier to slightly flex your feet at the same time that you flex your calves.)
- Next, move up to your *thighs*. Flex your thigh muscles as you breathe slowly, fully and deeply to a count of four. Hold your breath for a moment. Then slowly exhale to a count of four as you relax your thighs.
- Continue up your body to your *hips and buttocks*. Flex the muscles in your hips and bottom as you breathe slowly, fully and deeply to a count of four. Hold your breath for a moment. Then slowly exhale to a count of four as you relax these muscles.
- Now focus on your *back and stomach*. Flex and stretch the muscles in your back and then your stomach as you breathe slowly, fully and deeply to a count of four. Hold your breath for a moment. Then slowly exhale to a count of four as you relax your back and stomach.
- Move to your *chest and shoulders*. Flex the muscles in your chest and shoulders as you breathe slowly, fully and deeply to a count of four. (You may find it helpful to roll your shoulders. And you may notice that you've been holding a lot of tension in this part of your body.) Hold your breath for a moment. Then slowly exhale to a count of four as you relax these muscles. At this point, if it feels beneficial to do your chest and especially your shoulders again, please do so.
- Continue to your *arms*. Flex and stretch the muscles in your upper arms and forearms as you breathe slowly, fully and deeply to a count of four. Hold your breath for a moment. Then slowly exhale to a count of four as you relax your arms.
- Now move to your *hands and fingers*. Flex the muscles in your hands and fingers—spreading your fingers as wide as possible—as you breathe slowly, fully and deeply to a count of four. Hold your breath

for a moment. Then slowly exhale to a count of four as you relax your hands and fingers and return them to where they were resting.

- Next, focus on the muscles in your *neck*. Start with your head facing forward. Then stretch your neck muscles by slowly moving your face and head to the right as far as is comfortable, toward your right shoulder. Your head should be facing to your right. Breathe slowly, fully and deeply to a count of four as you do this. Hold your breath for a moment while facing to the right. Then, as you exhale slowly to a count of four, move your head back until you're facing forward. Next, as you breathe slowly, fully and deeply to a count of four, slowly stretch your neck as you move your face and head as far to the left as is comfortable. Hold your breath for a moment with your head over your left shoulder. Then, as you exhale slowly to a count of four, return your head to its previous position until you're facing forward. You may want to repeat this exercise for your neck.

- Now move to your *face*. Breathe slowly, deeply and fully to a count of four as you gently scrunch up your face as tight as is comfortable. You can start by moving the muscles in your cheeks around your nose and then pull up the muscles in your chin as you pull the muscles in your forehead down. When you hold your breath for a moment, you may be surprised at how much tension you've been holding in your facial muscles. Now relax your muscles as you exhale slowly to a count of four. You may want to do this more than once, focusing on different parts of your face, such as your forehead, nose, cheeks, lips and mouth. Take your time.

- Finally, focus on your *scalp*. You may not be able to flex or move your scalp very much, so try gently wiggling the muscles in your ears and raising your eyebrows as high as you can. This should move your scalp around a little. As with your face, you may notice that you've been holding stress in the skin around your skull. Breathe slowly, deeply and fully to a count of four during this process. Then hold your breath for a moment. Now relax your scalp, ears and forehead muscles as you slowly exhale to a count of four. And, like your face, neck and shoulders, you may want to do this more than once. Take your time as you release tension and feel it melting away.

As you move to each part of your body, remember to take a slow, full, deep breath when you flex or stretch, and slowly exhale as you relax. If you can't flex or stretch, then slightly move that part of your body as you slowly and deeply inhale to a count of four. Then slowly exhale to a count of four as you relax. If you can't move that part of your body, then try to bring awareness to it as you slowly inhale and exhale.

There are no set rules here, so if you feel certain parts of your body would benefit from doing a particular exercise a few times, please go ahead. Or if you want to group muscles together, like your feet and calves or arms and hands, or if you want to skip parts, it's okay. You're in charge. But if you do the entire routine as presented above slowly and with intention, there's a chance that you'll fall asleep before you get to your scalp.

To Sum Up

- When we experience a surprising or traumatic event, our brain naturally formulates an account that describes what happened and why in order to make sense of what occurred. The story we tell ourselves is called a "narrative."
- In the mid–1960s, Elisabeth Kübler-Ross started researching how terminally ill people are affected by the knowledge that they are going to die and, ultimately, how it affects those left behind. She eventually wrote the best-selling book *On Death and Dying* (1969). Her five stages of grief—denial, anger, bargaining, depression, and acceptance—are now universally accepted.
- New research reveals that grief is an ongoing process that may or may not end. Studies in nations such as China reveal that when the bereaved continue a relationship with their dead ancestors, they suffer less long-term distress than mourning Americans do.
- People with a past positive point of view judge, evaluate and react to things in the present moment through memories of happy experiences. Overall, people who have a past positive viewpoint tend to be less anxious than those with a past negative perspective. They also tend to be happier, healthier, and more successful.
- People who skew toward a past negative point of view judge, evaluate, and react to things in the present moment through memories of unhappy experiences. They are stuck, facing backward, perpetually replaying what happened in their mind. People with post-traumatic stress or major depression usually have a high past negative ZTPI score.
- Grief is similar to post-traumatic stress in that it can be deeply embedded in the brain. Just like post-traumatic stress, grief isn't

located in any one area because our memories (as well as sight, smell, hearing, physical sensation and pain) are all stored in different parts of the brain. Thus, sad or painful thoughts can be triggered whenever one of these senses reminds us of our loss.

- The more we practice replacing past negative thoughts with past positive recollections, the easier it becomes and, eventually, the better and more in control we'll feel.
- Being mindful of our thoughts, especially the negative thoughts holding us back from doing what we want or need to do, is the first step on our path to well-being.
- Practicing a breathing technique helps clear our minds to aid in our search for good memories. It helps us refocus from the constant chatter in our mind to the breaths we frequently take for granted.
- Recalling past positive memories by using as many of the five senses as possible strengthens the memories and makes them easier to access. These memories are vital in lowering a past negative time perspective mindset. This is accomplished by replacing a past negative thought with a past positive memory as soon as you are aware that the past negative is weighing you down.
- Nighttime, and especially bedtime, can be the most difficult time of day if you are grieving. Give yourself some space to relax by putting away work and your to-do list at least one hour before your bedtime routine begins. Turn off electronic devices thirty minutes before bedtime.
- Before you go to bed, taking a few moments to review the things you did during the day can boost self-esteem. By making a short list of what you need to do the next day, you won't have to stay awake, worrying about them, that night.
- The stress we feel throughout the day is held in our muscles. By practicing a muscle relaxation technique while lying in bed, we can help relieve the stress and pave the way for a more restful, rejuvenating night's sleep.

References

APA Staff. (2018). Stress effects on the body. *American Psychological Association*. https://www.apa.org/topics/stress/body.

Beck, J. (2015, August 10). Life's stories. *The Atlantic*. https://www.theatlantic.com/health/archive/2015/08/life-stories-narrative-psychology-redemption-mental-health/400796/.

Davidson, R.J., & McEwen, B.S. (2012). Social influences on neuroplasticity: Stress and interventions to promote well-being. *Nature Neuroscience, 15*, 689–95.

Eagleman, D. (2011). *Incognito: The secret lives of the brain.* New York, NY: Vintage.

Everplans Team. (n.d.). Thirteen perspectives on mourning and memorial events: Different religions have various approaches to mourning and memorial events. *Everplans.* https://www.everplans.com/articles/13-religious-perspectives-on-mourning-and-memorial-events.

Good Therapy Staff. (2018, May 20). When loss hurts: 6 physical effects of grief. *Good Therapy.* https://www.goodtherapy.org/blog/when-loss-hurts-6-physical-effects-of-grief-0520187.

Haley, E., & Williams, L. (2018, July 30). 17 types of grief every funeral director should know. *Funeral Friend.* http://thefuneralfriend.com/index.php/2018/07/30/17-types-of-grief-every-funeral-director-should-know/.

Juan, S. (2006, October 6). What are the most widely practiced religions of the world? *The Register.* https://www.theregister.com/2006/10/06/the_odd_body_religion/.

Krull, E. (2022). Grief by the numbers: Facts and statistics. *The Recovery Village.* https://www.therecoveryvillage.com/mental-health/grief/grief-statistics/.

Kübler-Ross, E. (2014). *On death and dying: What the dying have to teach doctors, nurses, clergy, and their own families.* New York, NY: Scribner (reprint edition).

Kübler-Ross, E., & Kessler, D. (2014). *On grief and grieving: Finding the meaning of grief through the five stages.* New York, NY: Scribner (reprint edition).

National Library of Medicine. (n.d.). Exhibit 1.3-4: DSM-5 diagnostic criteria for PTSD. *National Institute of Health.* https://www.ncbi.nlm.nih.gov/books/NBK207191/box/part1_ch3.box16/.

O'Rourke, M. (2010, January 24). Good grief: Is there a better way to be bereaved? *New Yorker.* https://www.newyorker.com/magazine/2010/02/01/good-grief.

Sword, R.K.M., & Zimbardo, P. (2014, April 29). This is your brain. *Psychology Today.* https://www.psychologytoday.com/us/blog/the-time-cure/201404/is-your-brain.

Taylor-Desir, M. (2022, November). What is post-traumatic stress disorder? *American Psychiatric Association.* https://www.psychiatry.org/patients-families/ptsd/what-is-ptsd

World Data. (n.d.). Spread of Christianity. https://www.worlddata.info/religions/christianity.php#.

Zimbardo, P., & Boyd, J. (2008). *The time paradox: The new psychology of time that will change your life.* London, UK: Rider.

Zimbardo, P., Sword, R.M., & Sword, R.K.M. (2012). *The time cure.* Hoboken, NJ: Wiley.

Zisook, S., & Shear, K. (2009). Grief and bereavement: What psychiatrists need to know. *World Psychiatry, 8*(2), 67–74.

Then, someone at my side says,
"There, she is gone."
Gone where?
Gone from my sight.
That is all.

—Henry Van Dyke

THREE

The Present

When writing this section, we realized that explaining the past (what has already happened) and the future (what will occur) is much easier than explaining the present. One definition of the present that we discovered was a single word: *Now*. But how do you explain "now"? To paraphrase David Seaburn, PhD: Max Planck, the originator of quantum theory and Nobel Prize (Physics) recipient in 1918, created a formula suggesting that the "present" lasts 10 to the -43 seconds, which is how long it takes a photon to do something we don't really understand. Other scientists have based their definition of the present on electrochemical brain activity and figure the present moment lasts about 200 milliseconds.

So, let's just say that the present is that time between the past and the future, which means that (at least physically) we are forever in the present. But as we've seen in the previous chapter, our minds can travel to the past, as well as to whatever future we create with our consciousness, even though our bodies are still here, in the present. That's pretty amazing when you think about it—that our minds and bodies can be in different time zones simultaneously.

Further, while we live in the present—and as you've probably noted in your ZTPI scores—we can experience things to varying degrees of negativity and positivity. In this chapter, we'll be focusing on present fatalism, which is a negative mindset that is easy to slip into when we're grieving. How can we not? Our lives are different. Now there's a big, gaping hole that was once filled by our loved one. What can we do to feel whole again? Well, toward the end of this chapter we've included numerous exercises for you to try out to replace present fatalism with selected, more upbeat present hedonism. We hope you'll adopt some of the suggestions and use them whenever you find yourself sliding down that slippery slope of depression or anxiety.

We'll be covering many subjects in this chapter. Some of them aren't usually discussed, and they may make you feel uncomfortable. But we think these topics are important ones to share. Our hope is that you will come to have a better understanding of what happened and why, or be better prepared for what may come, or learn from how other people handled difficult situations in that moment. So buckle up. We'll start with what is fast becoming a growing phenomenon in our nation.

Caregivers

We are going to take a deep dive into this fundamental topic because as the population ages, a steadily increasing number of people are providing care who aren't health care professionals. In fact, at some point in their lifetime, it's highly likely that one in three people will be a caregiver. The information we're sharing is for nonprofessionals who have or are caring for a terminally ill loved one. But we encourage all to read about what happens between a caregiver and their beloved, as well as the side effects experienced and some ways to help a caregiver be most effective.

• • •

Whether experiencing anticipatory grief (which occurs before the expected death of someone to whom we're close due to illness or injury) or actively grieving the recent loss of a loved one, being or having been their caregiver may compound the grief we feel. To be clear, a caregiver is anyone who provides help to another person in need, such as an ill spouse or partner, a disabled child, or an aging relative. But most family members who care for their relatives don't identify themselves as "caregivers." This may be because for most nonprofessional caregivers, being there when a loved one needs you is a core value[1]; it's something you want to do.

It's important to acknowledge that the relationship you and your loved one had (i.e., child/parent, spouses, life partners, siblings, friends) changed when you became the caregiver. Yes, you are and will always be their child, parent, spouse, life partner, brother/sister, or friend. But your relationship has transitioned and there was a marked shift, possibly a role reversal. The person you care for may feel robbed of the part they once played in your life. This happens sometimes in marital and life partnerships, as well as parent/child relationships. Meanwhile, you may feel like you instantly became the parent of your beloved. The expectations of what your loved one contributed to your relationship in the past versus what

---

1. A core value is an internal compass of personal principles or morals that guide you in your decision making.

they are able to contribute now will likewise need adjusting. As time progresses, additional modifications may be necessary.

This major adjustment and the flood of emotions it brings are normal. If your loved one is still alive, you can discern whether this subject needs to be discussed openly; it may be obvious and not require mentioning. Or your loved one may not want to address the change in your roles because it's too emotionally painful. But if they are expending too much physical or mental energy trying to maintain a relationship that stresses their mind or body, consider telling them it's okay to let go of their past responsibilities. You've got this. Their energy is too precious to use on tasks that someone else can readily do. They should save their strength for their most important tasks. And your love is greater than anything that they think needs to be expressed physically. (More on this topic later in this chapter.)

If you were the main caregiver for the deceased, you may feel a deeper sort of grief because you lost your loved one *and* your purpose: being their constant companion and taking care of them. After some time has passed, you may feel a sense of relief or freedom. This is also normal. Unfortunately, feelings of guilt can piggyback on this feeling of independence, holding you down and hampering your grieving process. If you are identifying with this situation, ideally this chapter will help you overcome feeling this way.

Caregiver Stress

We're including stress in this section because even if your caregiving days are over, depending on how much time has passed, you may still be experiencing caregiver stress—that is, the emotional and physical stress of caregiving. Your focus is on your loved one, and you may be unaware that your own health and well-being are simultaneously deteriorating. To add to your stress, family members may be critical of your caregiving without fully understanding all you have to do, or they may burden you further by not offering help. They may feel that visiting for an hour or two every few weeks is equivalent to your 24/7 in-person caregiving. It isn't. So don't listen. For whatever the reason, you took this task on, they didn't, and you're doing the best you can.

But to cut them some slack—and also explain why some people might stay away—their criticism may be rooted in their feelings about illness. They may be uncomfortable or fearful being near a sick or dying person. Perhaps it's upsetting to see someone who played a prominent role in their life, someone who was once vigorous, deteriorate before their eyes. It might remind them of their own mortality and how this may very well happen to them one day in the future, which is too much to bear.

Here are the signs of caregiver stress:

- Feeling overwhelmed or constantly worried
- Feeling tired often
- Getting too much sleep or not enough sleep
- Gaining or losing weight
- Becoming easily irritated or angry
- Losing interest in activities that were enjoyable
- Feeling sad
- Having frequent headaches, bodily pain or other physical problems
- Abusing alcohol or drugs, including prescription medications

It's normal to feel angry, frustrated, and overwhelmed as a caregiver. But it's crucial to be aware that too much stress, especially over a long period of time, can harm your health. You've probably noted that some of these symptoms are also signs of depression, anxiety, and trauma/post-traumatic stress. Understandably, as the caregiver of a loved one, you're more likely to experience depression and anxiety. In addition, you may not get enough sleep or physical activity, or perhaps you are not eating a balanced diet. You may not be able to do much about this problem right now. But these things increase your risk of medical issues, such as heart disease and diabetes. We don't mean to scold you. We care about you and want you to take care of yourself as much as possible. It is essential to being an effective caregiver.

Rick and Rose: Circle of Support

For months after his initial cancer diagnosis, Rick and I were at a cancer treatment center far from home. The center had a multistory temporary housing facility for outpatients and caregivers to rent during their loved one's treatment. It was a few blocks away from the treatment center. At the end of the first day when Rick was admitted as an inpatient, a nurse kindly took me aside and said it was a good idea for me to leave. When I asked why, she shared that we weren't in for a sprint; we were in for a marathon, and I needed to get as much rest as possible. The nurse and I both looked at a dozing Rick. Although loath to leave him, the nurse's wisdom reverberated somewhere deep inside me. I nodded, leaned in to give Rick a kiss and whispered that I'd see him in the morning.

Three: The Present

It was twilight as I walked back to our new abode to spend the first of many, many nights by myself. I noticed under a streetlight in the mostly empty housing facility parking lot a group of people, both men and women of different ages, standing or sitting in a loose circle. Those sitting were on upside-down empty paint buckets or folding chairs. Some smoked cigarettes, others drank beverages, and one woman was drying her tears with a paper dinner napkin. They greeted me and asked whether I was a caregiver. When I said I was, they asked me to join them. They were all staying at the hospital's housing facility.

They met haphazardly at around this time in this space. Some were family members, but most were spouses. They took this time—maybe fifteen to twenty minutes—to update each other on their loved one's status. On rare occasions they would share bits and pieces of their "other, normal" lives. These caregivers were from across the United States; Rick and I had come the farthest, as we were from Hawai'i. Some had been here multiple times with their loved ones. Others had been here for weeks or months.

Members of the impromptu caregivers group came and went as their loved ones were released or passed away. Sometimes only two or three people would show up. At other times there were as many as twelve. I don't recall any of us sharing our names. We weren't at the facility for ourselves, and so we seldom spoke about ourselves. Our lives were consumed by what was happening to our loved ones, how they fared, and what we could do for them. But we brought comfort and support to each other, as each of us knew what the others were going through during these incredibly hard times. We grieved for the loss of the lives we had once known with our loved ones when they were healthy, but this was only hinted at and never directly addressed.

Early one morning, as I walked to the treatment facility to be with Rick for the day, I caught up with another caregiver. She hadn't been at the parking lot meeting for days, causing us to think she and her husband had gone home. She told me she had suffered a ministroke or transient ischemic attack and chalked it up to stress! She had been in a hospital for two days but felt better and was anxious to resume her caregiver duties. Then she told me that shortly before Rick and I had arrived, another caregiver had suffered a massive heart attack and died, leaving behind his wife to undergo cancer treatment on her own. After hearing this news, the wind was knocked out of me for a few minutes. I sat in the lobby of the treatment center, gathering my thoughts before going up to spend the day with Rick. I felt such intense sadness about the irony of the situation: the supposedly healthy spouse died while the "unhealthy" spouse was left on her own. I had to take better care of myself. I couldn't allow that to happen to Rick.

Help for Caregiver Stress

Even the most resilient people are strained by the stress of the physical and emotional demands of being a caregiver. So it's important to take advantage of the many resources available to help you provide care for your beloved. This includes self-care for *you* because, by caring for yourself, you'll be able to care longer and better for someone else. Here are some tips to help you manage caregiver stress:

- *Accept help.* This task may be very difficult for some caregivers, as they don't want to be a bother or intrude in other people's lives. Plus, they might think no one can do what they do for their loved one better than them. This is a recipe for quick caregiver burnout. So prepare a list of ways that others can help you, and let the helper choose what he or she would like to do. This can take the form of running errands, picking up groceries, making a meal, or spending an hour or two sitting with the person you care for so you can have a break. Keep your list updated.
- *Focus on what you can do.* No one is a perfect caregiver. So try not to feel guilty when you can't do everything. You're doing your best and making the best decisions you can when they need to be made.
- *Set realistic goals.* You may be the sort of person who can't say "no," but it may be time to start doing so. Say "no" to requests that are draining, such as hosting gatherings or attending events. Prioritize and make lists. Establish a daily and weekly routine. Divide large tasks into smaller portions so you can start and complete things one at a time.
- *Connect.* Find out about caregiving resources in your community. Services such as transportation, meal delivery or housekeeping may be available. Perhaps you can designate a helper to run point on researching such possibilities for you.
- *Join a support group.* A support group can provide validation and encouragement, as well as problem-solving strategies for difficult situations. People in support groups understand what you may be going through. A support group can also be a good place to create meaningful friendships.
- *Seek social support.* Make an effort to stay connected with family and friends who can offer emotional support and try to avoid toxic relationships that drain you of the confidence and strength

you need. Set aside time each week for connecting with those who appreciate and support you in your efforts as a caregiver, even if it's just a phone or virtual talk or a walk with a friend.

- *Set personal health goals.* For example, find time to be physically active on most days of the week, eat a healthy diet and drink plenty of water.
- *Establish a good sleep routine.* Many caregivers have issues with sleeping. Not getting quality sleep over a long period of time can cause health issues. If the sleep routine you are trying to establish isn't working and you're having trouble getting a good night's rest, talk to your doctor. If caregiving duties keep you up at night, see whether it's possible to get a night nurse to give you time for the sleep you need to be at your best (see below).
- *See your doctor.* Keep up with recommended vaccinations and screenings. Make sure to tell your doctor that you're a caregiver. Don't hesitate to mention any concerns or symptoms you have.

Depending on the services provided in your community and the type of health care your loved one receives, the following suggestions might not be feasible for some caregivers. But if these services are available and you need a break, check out:

- *In-home respite*: Health care aides come to your home to provide companionship, nursing services or both. Hospice can provide this service.
- *Adult care centers and programs*: Some centers provide care for both older adults and young children, and the two groups may spend time together.
- *Short-term nursing homes*: Some assisted living homes, memory care homes and nursing homes accept people needing care for short stays while caregivers are away.

If you're feeling isolated, frustrated and depressed, don't struggle on your own. Contact your local Area Agency on Aging (AAA) to learn about services in your community. You can find your local AAA online (https://eldercare.acl.gov/Public/About/Aging_Network/AAA.aspx) or in the government section of your telephone directory.

Phil: My Beautiful Sister, Vera

I was the oldest of four children in the Zimbardo family living in the Bronx, New York City. Next in line came brothers George and Don, with little Vera as the youngest, six years my junior. She was really a beautiful child and continued to be so as she grew older. Many people thought that she looked like the Italian film actress Sophia Loren, but even more beautiful. When Vera later displayed talent for painting, I arranged for her to go to an art school, where she eventually married her teacher, John Massimino. They soon had a daughter, Neva, who was a delightful and beautiful child. John's family had a villa on the Italian island of Capri, where his family would vacation every summer. I enjoyed several visits there with the entire Massimino family.

Unfortunately, Vera developed breast cancer at a time when effective medical treatments were not yet well developed. She came back to the States, had that one breast removed, and tried to stay upbeat, with me at her side, teaching her self-hypnosis both to minimize pain and to stay positive. Sadly, the dreaded cancer soon spread to her other breast, which also had to be removed. I spent as much time as I could with Vera while also counseling her husband John. It was a time in my career when I traveled overseas often to give invited lectures in foreign countries. However, I always made time to visit the local cathedral to light candles and say prayers in support of my beautiful sister. Nevertheless, cancer won over all these many prayers; Vera died at the youthful age of forty-one years. I should add that both of my parents, George and Margaret, had died of cancer a few years earlier, when they were only sixty-eight years old. However, what killed them was heavy cigarette tobacco smoking, which Vera never ever did. I still grieve over the untimely deaths of my beloved parents and darling sister, Vera.

Hospice Care

When it is no longer possible to cure a serious illness, or if your loved one chooses not to undergo certain treatments, their physician may refer them to hospice care. Hospice is provided for a person with a terminal illness whose doctor believes they have six months or less to live if the illness runs its natural course. Hospice was specially designed for this situation. It focuses on the care, comfort, and quality of life for your loved one, in addition to providing support for the family. Although attempts to cure them cease, other medical care continues if it is judged to be helpful. For instance, if your loved one has high blood pressure, he or she will still get medicine for that condition.

Sometimes loved ones or their caregivers don't take advantage of hospice care as soon as they could, causing all involved to miss out on the many ways hospice can really help them. Other than not knowing about hospice services, this can happen when the loved one or the caregiver is in denial about their situation. The patient may think they can "beat this," even when they've been told there is nothing more to be done, or the caregiver may think they don't need the help. This misunderstanding may cause them to wait too long, so that their loved one may be too close to death for hospice to make a difference. Conversely, and sadly, some people are not eligible for hospice care soon enough to receive its full benefit. Starting hospice early may be able to provide months of meaningful care and quality time with loved ones.

Since hospice is an approach to care and not a single organization, it can be offered in two different settings: at home or in a facility such as a hospital, a nursing home, or a hospice center. Experts—doctors, nurses, social workers, trained volunteers and spiritual advisors—work together with the dying person, the caregiver, and/or the family to provide medical, emotional, and spiritual support. A member of the hospice team visits regularly, and someone is always available by phone—twenty-four hours a day, seven days a week. Hospice costs may be covered by Medicare and other insurance companies. If you or your loved one needs hospice care, check to see whether insurance will cover your situation.

Although hospice provides a lot of support, the day-to-day care of a person dying at home is usually provided by family and close friends. The hospice team coaches family members on how to care for the dying person and even provides respite care when caregivers need a break. Respite care can be for as short as a few hours or as long as several weeks. Hospice recipients are more likely to have their pain controlled and less likely to undergo tests or be given medicines they don't need, compared with people who don't use hospice care.

If your loved one lives longer than six months, their doctor can certify that they are still close to dying, in which case Medicare will continue to pay for hospice services. It's also possible to leave hospice care for a while and return later if the doctor still believes your loved one has less than six months to live.

Rick and Rose:
Everything Everywhere All at Once

Picking up where we left off in Chapter Two, eleven months after diagnosis—*I followed Rick's new primary care physician (PCP) into the hallway, where he asked how I was holding up. Reeling from the meandering way he had broken the news that there was no hope for Rick, I ignored his question and asked for the results of the latest computed tomography (CT) scans of Rick's body. Even though Rick had endured radiation, chemotherapy and radical surgery, the cancer had spread to his lungs, brain and elsewhere. Putting emotions to the side—I could fall apart later in the shower—I took a deep breath and pragmatically asked how long he thought Rick might have to live. He shook his head and said it was impossible to tell, but if he guessed, maybe Rick would make it to the holidays. Maybe not. I nodded. It was spring. Maybe we had nine months more until Christmas. Maybe less.*

Then he asked again how I was doing. I was honest, telling him I was overwhelmed with responsibilities: being Rick's primary caregiver, overseeing our clinic (Richard M. Sword, PhD, Inc., which specialized in PTS) and household, getting ready for our youngest to graduate from high school, and preparing for her to attend university on the East Coast. He asked whether I had considered having Rick live in a nursing home; he could write up the paperwork that day. I was appalled. There was no way Rick was going anywhere other than our home. I explained to the doctor that no matter how hard life was right now, I knew it wasn't going to be this way forever and time with Rick was precious. Then he asked whether I wanted antidepressants or antianxiety medications. I know he meant well. It was his way of being kind and acknowledging what I had just shared. My PCP, knowing my stress level, had recently asked the same thing. Thanking him, I declined his offer, just as I had hers for such medications.

On the way home, Rick wanted to discuss what his doctor meant about taxes and the Big Guy upstairs. Rick was a brilliant man, one of the most intelligent people I had ever met. He was an excellent psychologist and instructor. But intelligence doesn't dictate how we react to new situations. From the very beginning when Rick was first diagnosed, he had been in denial about the seriousness of his cancer. This would also prove to be true for a few family members as well as some of our friends. In our relationship, Rick and I were honest with each other. I was not going to lie to him now. I told him everything that could be done for him had been done. There were no more procedures, and his cancer had spread.

From that point forward, we would spend nearly every moment together. For the first of many times, he took hold of my hand and said, "I don't want to go; I just want to hang out with you."

"Me, too; I just want to hang out with you," I responded as I squeezed his hand tight. And we did, until we didn't anymore.

The Vultures in the Room

This topic may be forbidden for some to discuss openly, because it's considered private and may reveal hidden dysfunction in familial relationships, especially at a delicate and distressing time. But we'd be remiss if we didn't devote a section in this book to this unfortunate but common occurrence. There is no subtle way to put this, so we'll address it head on: The following is about the greed displayed by some family members, including in-laws, for the material and financial goods of the deceased, and why this phenomenon takes place. These kinfolk have been likened to vultures because of their propensity to prey on and exploit others.

Grief counselors and therapists hear innumerable reports of this conflict happening in what outsiders perceive to be well-functioning families. You've probably heard stories, too. But what most people on the outside may not realize if they haven't experienced it is that this infighting causes additional stress and heartbreak for the grieving spouse, parent, sibling or executor who is left to handle the property (or "estate"). Some family members of the deceased can harbor feelings of avarice, while others experience shock, anger or resentment due to the covetous behavior of their kin. To add to the mix, predatory in-laws are sometimes to blame as they pressure their vulnerable, grieving spouse to don the mantle of greed and take advantage of the mourning person in charge. The pain of grief can be compounded when there is no will (which we address later in this chapter) or executor appointed, leaving the estate to probate and a free-for-all among discordant heirs.

The grieving family undergoing this scenario may think they are keeping things under wraps. But people, including relatives, like to talk—and gossip—and word can spread like wildfire. Let's presume that the deceased doesn't care about this world anymore, but people outside the family are watching, sometimes with great interest. They wonder: Will this happen in *my* family? With a little knowledge, you might be able to get a good idea of how likely this possibility may be. And then you can take steps to avert it as best you can in the future.

Parents, you might not like to hear this, but you may be the primary cause of covetous behavior in your child(ren). Vulture, you may not be able to hear this because you don't believe you are at fault. At the root of this conduct are *narcissism* and *feelings of entitlement*. This situation emerges in the original family when children are made to compete against each other. It's reinforced when parents insist that family comes first, no matter what (meaning that everyone needs to tolerate the abusive behavior of one child against another just because they are family). Narcissistic children are enabled by their parents when parents excuse their bad behavior, which makes for toxic relationships. Perhaps you've heard the nonsensical defense "That's just [Fill-in-the-blank] being [Fill-in-the-blank]," which is an all-encompassing justification for misbehavior and misdemeanors. Parents make the situation worse when they insist the other sibling(s) "be nice" to the narcissistic brother or sister.

A child's narcissistic characteristics are usually evident when they are young. They like to keep score and feel compelled to outdo their sibling(s). They will separate family members and play them against each other. As children, narcissists believe they deserve more of a parent's attention. It's not surprising that children brought up in narcissistic homes rarely feel connected to one another as adults.

As adults, narcissists continue believing that they deserve more of their parents' attention, along with their money. But when the time comes, they show no interest and can't be bothered to help care for their parents. Adult siblings can become confused and understandably angry when their narcissistic sibling is abusive to them or a parent. Typically, the narcissist will "gaslight" their prey by flipping the situation and accusing the victim of being abusive. (*Note:* According to the *Oxford English Dictionary*, gaslighting is "manipulat[ing] (a person) by psychological means into questioning his or her own sanity.")

Crash Course in Narcissistic Personality Symptoms

Although we've written extensively about narcissistic personality disorder in books and articles, our focus was on adults. Fortunately, Fern Schumer Chapman (*Brothers, Sisters, Strangers*, 2021) has compiled a wealth of information on narcissistic siblings. She created the following lists of narcissistic behaviors and their effects on the abused:

- Changing the rules; "moving the goal posts" to benefit themselves
- Lacking empathy; never recognizing the needs of others
- Consistently being entitled and arrogant
- Altering reality to their benefit: defending or rationalizing self-serving behavior; deflecting blame; lying to exaggerate their own achievements
- Gaslighting to persuade others that they're mistaken in their perceptions

- "Shape-shifting" to misrepresent personal traits or an entire identity at will
- Manipulating others to their advantage
- Engaging in cruel behaviors to obtain advantage or just to inflict misery
- Triangulating; pitting people against each other
- Belittling, invalidating, and ignoring those they consider inferior [which can be almost everyone else]
- Monopolizing conversations; demanding constant attention
- Disrespecting boundaries; feeling entitled that they needn't comply with others' wishes
- Betraying confidence
- Launching "campaigns" against others: making themselves look perfect and their sibling look like the "crazy" one
- Competing so relentlessly that the jealousy and rivalry between adult siblings leads the non-narcissistic sibling to give up on spending time together
- Avoiding responsibility; blaming others; apologizing rarely (if ever)
- Taking advantage of others with cunning style and charm

Those who have experienced narcissistic abuse often struggle with the following:

- Confusion
- Anxiety
- Self-blame
- Self-doubt
- Helplessness
- Rumination
- Grief

• • •

Religions and Spiritual Practices: How We Mourn—Part 3

In this section, we'll explore the mourning practices of three of the five largest religions. Hinduism is believed to have started in the Indus Valley, near modern-day Pakistan, between 2300 BCE and 1500 BCE. However, many Hindus believe their faith has always existed. Unlike other religions, Hinduism has no single founder but is instead a fusion of various beliefs. By contrast, Islam started in Mecca, in modern-day Saudi Arabia, during the time of the prophet Muhammad's life. Hence, scholars generally date the establishment of Islam to the sixth/seventh centuries CE, making it the youngest of the major world religions. Dating back nearly four thousand years, Judaism is the world's oldest monotheistic religion. Followers of Judaism believe in one God who revealed himself through ancient prophets.

HINDUISM

The Hindu period of mourning lasts thirteen days, beginning with the cremation of the deceased. During this time the family remains at home, receives visitors, and observes certain rituals, which may vary from one community to another. Often the departed loved one's photo is featured in a prominent place and adorned with a flower garland. The day after cremation, the oldest male in the family (Karta) collects the ashes. According to tradition, the ashes should be released in the Ganges River. For families who live outside of India, there are companies that will ship the remains to India for this purpose. However, other rivers are now becoming acceptable as well. Throughout the period of mourning, the rite of Preta-Karma will be performed. This practice assists the disembodied spirit of the departed loved one in obtaining a new body for reincarnation. One year after the death, a memorial ritual (sraddha) and a feast will honor the departed family member. In some traditions, the family does not participate in festivals or celebrations for this first year, until after the sraddha has been observed.

ISLAM

The Islamic faith maintains a firm belief in the afterlife, and mourners find comfort in their understanding that death is a transition rather than a finality of life. Tears are expected, but Muslims strive to remain reserved and dignified in their mourning, finding comfort in prayer, readings from the Qur'an, meditation and reflection. The funeral (Salat ul Janazah) is actually a prayer service, petitioning God to forgive any sins committed by the departed loved one. While Islam demands no specific dress code, clothing is customarily conservative, favoring darker colors, with women wearing long skirts, high necklines, and headscarves. Shoes are removed during the funeral (and often while visiting some homes as well). Mourners may continue to pray together following the burial, during which time food and other necessities are provided for the immediate family, who may continue to receive comforting visitors for three days. The period of mourning for a widow is four months and ten days, during which time her basic needs are taken care of by family and friends. She does not generally leave home, and any interaction with men who may be eligible for marriage should be restricted. Grief is assuaged with the knowledge that life may be short, but all belongs to Allah, and a merciful God will ideally one day unite those who mourn a loss with their departed loved one once more.

JUDAISM

In the Jewish faith, there are two periods of mourning. The first is Shiva (seven), which takes place during the week following the funeral. During this time the family comes together daily to mourn and pray and to be available to receive guests. The Shiva candle is lit on the first day and will burn for the entire week. The family does not go to work or maintain their normal schedule of activities. The second period of mourning is Sheloshim (thirty), which lasts until the thirtieth day after the funeral. During this time mourners may resume much of their daily routine, but they will continue to recite the Mourner's Kaddish. At the end of Shloshim, the official period of mourning is over, except for those who are grieving the loss of a parent, in which case it will continue for one year. Two memorials are observed every year, one of which is on the evening before the anniversary of the death, when the yahrzeit candle is lit; the candle burns for twenty-four hours, and the Mourner's Kaddish is recited. Yizkor is a memorial prayer service held in the synagogue on Yom Kippur, Shemini Atzeret, and the last days of Passover and Shavuot. There is a rich heritage of Jewish traditions providing the comfort of specific instructions on all manner of concerns regarding the passing of a loved one.

• • •

Parents, Children, Narcissists

The narcissist you know may engage in some or all of the behaviors mentioned previously. If you are a narcissist, you may be able to alter your behavior, depending on the severity of your condition. It's possible for some narcissists to change if they are ready to accept responsibility, are able to see things from someone else's perspective, and are willing to reflect on their negative behavior. Narcissism is a complex personality trait, and, for many, there is no cure. However, therapy can help. Ironically, at the root of narcissism is low self-esteem. By building up self-esteem in a healthy way and learning to focus on more realistic expectations of others, narcissists can improve. But again, this only works if the narcissist is sincerely willing to make a change.

The treatment for narcissistic personality disorder is talk therapy, or psychotherapy. To quote our friends at Mayo Clinic, in therapy, one will:

- Learn to relate better with others so your relationships are closer, more enjoyable and more rewarding.
- Understand the causes of your emotions and what drives you to compete, to distrust others, and to dislike others and possibly yourself.

The focus is to help you accept responsibility and learn to

- Accept and maintain real personal relationships and work together with co-workers.
- Recognize and accept your actual abilities, skills and potential so you can tolerate criticism or failures.
- Increase your ability to understand and manage your feelings.
- Understand and learn how to handle issues related to your self-esteem.
- Learn to set and accept goals that you can reach instead of wanting goals that are not realistic.

Therapy can be short term to help you manage during times of stress or crisis. Therapy also can be provided on an ongoing basis to help you achieve and maintain your goals. Often, including family members or others in therapy can be helpful.

There are no medicines specifically used to treat narcissistic personality disorder. But if you have symptoms of depression, anxiety or other conditions, medicines such as antidepressants or anti-anxiety medicines may be helpful.

When parents ignore unhealthy, abusive relationships between siblings and insist that family comes first, those relationships are at risk of estrangement. In some cases, the only solution for the non-narcissistic sibling is to end the sibling relationship or break away from the entire family in order to protect themselves from a toxic sibling's harmful conduct. If the non-narcissistic brother or sister decides to stay in the relationship, they should set firm boundaries and decide what behaviors they'll tolerate. Then, *if appropriate* (because you may decide it's not wise to discuss your plans with others, as doing so might create more problems), let the narcissistic brother or sister—and again, if appropriate, your parent(s)—know the boundaries and decide on a consequence. If the pernicious sibling violates the boundary, enforce the consequence. Another approach that may work is a narrowly defined relationship. This can be accomplished by limiting exposure and maintaining a superficial relationship with the hurtful sibling.

Parents, your own experience and observations will inform you as to whether you raised a narcissist. The information in this section might confirm your findings. It probably wasn't your intention to prefer one child over another; you may think you were protecting your child for some reason. And if you're in denial, you may not believe your narcissist is one. But if one of your children is narcissistic, beware that relationship problems between your children in the future will likely occur, assuming there aren't already issues between them. (FYI: There is a good chance your narcissist is male, as a thirty-year study of more than 475,000 participants revealed that men—7.7 percent—are more likely to be narcissistic than women—4.8 percent.)

The Importance of Wills

Another matter that ties in with the above discussion has to do with wills. It is common for family members to discover that the deceased does not have a will. Likewise, it's not unusual for one parent to have a will but not the other. Recently we were told of a situation in which an older man, who had a will and left everything to his wife, died. His adult daughter, the executor of his will, went to help her mother with the funeral arrangements when her mother suddenly died—without a will. Like many surviving spouses, having a will drawn up was on her mother's list of things to do, but she ran out of time. As this book is written, the daughter is having great difficulty as she deals with the cumulative grief of losing both parents in a very short amount of time while trying to navigate the legal shambles in which she finds herself. To add to the mess, she has a narcissistic brother who feels entitled to everything. So, parents, don't do this to your children.

No matter if you have one or more children, there is something you can do to prevent some of the above difficulties from happening. Get your affairs in order as soon as possible; the more ironclad your documents, the better. If you are a person of means, you and your spouse may already have a personal attorney and last will and testaments for both of you. But if only one of you has a will, please look into providing the other with one soon.

If you are of modest means that preclude you from having such resources, a quick online search for a free *living will* (a medical form detailing your wishes if you are debilitated or close to death) and *last will and testament* (a legal document that explains your final wishes for the distribution of your assets when you die) can provide you with important information. Parents, when you make your wishes clear in a written document, you are helping those you leave behind. It's more than fine if you don't want to share what's in your will with your children in order to avoid possible jealousy and relationship problems. Any mystery as to what *you* want can remain until the reading of your will.

Rick and Rose:
The End of Physicality

It's hard to convey these personal experiences. But sharing parts of my own life as the wife and now widow of a once vibrant man offers a glimpse into a topic that people wonder about but rarely, if ever, discuss. Heads-up: This is very personal. It's intimate. I hope it's helpful.

Rick and I enjoyed a healthy sex life up until he was diagnosed. That changed overnight. Sex wasn't on the back burner—it was completely off the table. Arrangements were made at lightning speed, and within a few days we were at the cancer treatment center in the Midwest. Rick had radiation treatment and stayed for about two months. Although I was reluctant to leave him, after a couple of weeks I had to return home to hire a temporary psychologist for our clinic. Rick's sister came to be with him as my replacement, and then our oldest daughter stayed with him and brought him back to Hawai'i. He was home for about six weeks before we both returned to the cancer treatment center. But during that six-week time period we enjoyed each other intimately every night. We were like teenagers (sorry, kids).

Back in the Midwest, Rick underwent chemotherapy and radical surgery involving his esophagus and stomach. A feeding tube was placed in his abdomen. Rick was sick with pain and discomfort. Witnessing his suffering was beyond heart-wrenching. And so, in a way, I was grateful to be super busy. My time was divided between staying with Rick and meeting with staff for hours at the center when he was an inpatient and then caring for him when he was released and we were together at the housing complex. I was also trying to parent our children as well as run our clinic from afar, write columns for Psychology Today *with my coauthor Phil Zimbardo, and promote our recently published book,* The Time Cure. *Rick and I had been partners in every aspect of our lives. Now I knew I had to do my best to keep everything going without him and without making him feel that he was somehow failing or overburdening me. I'm not going to lie—it was a lot. Every night I fell into bed completely exhausted.*

When we returned home for good, Rick was looking forward to the time when he would feel well enough to try to have sex again. Honestly, I couldn't care less. It was as if a switch had been turned off in me. We were home for a few days when, being stubborn, he tried to stand by himself. He immediately got dizzy and fell. Fortunately, I was working from an adjoining room and heard him. He broke his hip. It was a bad break. Back to the hospital for another lengthy surgery and a two-week stay. Then into a rehabilitation center for what was supposed to be six weeks. But, against doctors' orders, Rick checked himself out after two weeks. Now his primary caregiver, I quickly learned how to act as his physical therapist before he came home. Friends helped us move Rick upstairs to our bedroom. I set everything up so all of his needs were met without Rick having to go downstairs for anything.

Two more months went by, and he felt he had recuperated enough to try to have sex. It didn't work. He tried. We tried. It was a no-go. Every couple of days we'd try. Every couple of days it didn't work. He was frustrated and disheartened. This went on for a month. It was now March, and we had just returned from the doctor telling us there was nothing more to be done for Rick. We tried for the last time that night. After a valiant attempt, he said in a teary voice, "What good am I if I can't please my wife? I might as well be dead." It broke my heart that he might have thought sex was the overarching connection that kept us together.

I knew whatever I said now was of paramount importance. I didn't want him to give up just because we couldn't make love. The sex act is, in itself, a primal affirmation of life force. What would it mean to him to know we had lost that forever? As I hugged him, my throat tight with emotion, face wet with tears, I assured him that our love was a powerful force and far greater than anything physical. I didn't love him because of sex. I loved him because of his soul. We were partners together. Always. It was time for us to stop putting energy toward frustrating fruitless efforts that made him feel bad about himself. I was content with our relationship and hoped he could be, too. We should cherish our time together. Eyes closed, cheeks damp, he smiled sadly and nodded.

Some friends asked how I could continue sleeping with Rick because he was hooked up to machines and would sweat profusely. (Chemotherapy and morphine can cause hot flashes and sweating; sheets should be changed frequently.) My response was always the same: How could I not? I loved this man, body and soul. We didn't have sex again. But once in a while we would reminisce and talk about how much fun we used to have in bed. It was a time in our life, like hiking Haleakala Crater, or surfing, or camping. We continued to be very affectionate—kissing, hugging, snuggling, sleeping closely together—until the day he died in late June.

· · ·

I'm not sure when I stopped beating myself up about making the decision to tell Rick there was nothing more to be done and to end our attempts to have sex. Maybe I never have. These efforts were extremely frustrating and depressing for both of us. The amount of energy it took— physical and mental—would leave Rick totally depleted. My head told me that being honest was the right thing to do to prepare us for what was to come. But a part of me kept wondering: If he didn't know, and we had continued to try, would he have lived longer? Did he give up after the devastating events of this particular day and night? Because he didn't live for the nine months we optimistically hoped for. He lasted only about another three months. Of course, there's no way of knowing. But I'll ask when I see him again one day. I have to believe I'll see him again one day, and I do because when I was very ill and near death myself about a year ago, I saw him. He was not far away, standing on a small hill, patiently waiting for me.

Bias Toward the Present

When people are biased toward living in a present time perspective, they aren't influenced by either past experiences or future deliberations. Their focus is on what's happening *now*. Some of these folks base their decisions on the inner forces and the outer pressures of their immediate stimulus condition: internal hormonal signals; feelings; senses such as sight, smell, and sounds; the attractiveness of the object of desire; and what others are insisting they do. For them, the answer to the question "If everyone else is jumping off a bridge, would you?" is a hedonistic "YES!" For other present-oriented people, it's possible their past—whether long ago or recent—was so negative that it spills over into their present, where everything is bleak and fatalistic. It's understandable that grieving people would score high in a bias toward the present, and from our grief work and research, it's typically fatalistic rather than hedonistic.

Present hedonists seek pleasure. Delayed gratification isn't in their vocabulary. Their mottos are "Carpe Diem!" "YOLO!" (you only live once), "If it feels good, do it!" and "Eat, drink and be merry!" For present hedonists, a delicious treat in the moment is worth two later on; they can't wait. They make decisions *now*, so they'll have another drink at the bar or party before driving home. And they'll hook up with someone they just met for casual sex. They'll do these things even though what they did in the past got them into trouble, like a car accident, or jail, or an unwanted pregnancy. They don't take their negative experiences into consideration when making decisions. They don't seem to learn from the past or worry much about tomorrow. They want what they want when they want it, end of story. Or so they think. (*Note:* Children and teenagers—and some young adults—are usually biased toward present hedonism. They are just learning how to traverse their world and lack the life experience it takes to make informed decisions.)

Present hedonism in moderation—*selected present hedonism*—is a good thing and is a goal we aim for in TPT. But too much of a good thing all the time can lead to feeling like we're stuck on an out-of-control bullet train—of addiction (alcohol, drug, food, gambling, internet, sex, shopping, video games). Because present hedonists actively search for pleasure, it's not surprising that they tend to be happier and more creative than their fatalistic peers.

Temporary Present Fatalism

When you're grieving, it's possible to have a *temporary present fatalistic* mindset. For example, if you had taken the ZTPI prior to your loss, when life was "normal," you may have scored high in, let's say, past positive and future time perspectives. But due to your current circumstances, your recent ZTPI scores indicate high present fatalism. This is understandable given what has happened and where you may find yourself: in the dark chasm of grief.

However, no one knows you better than you know yourself.

If you feel that you are *temporarily* experiencing present fatalism, then, as you read the rest of this section, it may not apply to your normal personality and time perspectives. But your current experience, as well as the information in this chapter, might help you better understand your grieving self as well as experience greater compassion for your fatalistic friends and family members. Also, the exercises at the end of this chapter can help you get back to your old self when you're ready.

If, however, you recently scored high in present fatalism and the following resonates with you, then the exercises in this chapter can help you gain time perspective balance by including some selected present hedonism in your life.

• • •

True *present fatalists* live in a very different present than their hedonistic counterparts. Some believe that everything is determined by fate, by external forces, or by religiously determined destiny. They see little to no need to spend time planning and plotting and considering behavioral options because the conclusion is already fated. Their motto is "What will be will be." They surrender all decision-making control to God or the universe, believing the outcome of each decision or problem is predetermined. This mindset can leave individuals feeling powerless and therefore pessimistic as well as cynical, which they may prefer to view as being "realistic."

While present fatalists believe their lives follow a fated plan over which they have little or no control, present hedonists desperately seek to overcontrol by indulging in immediate pleasure (frequently to avoid pain) without regard for the consequences. Both mindsets focus on the present situation instead of the past or the future.

A present time perspective orientation is understandable among those who have lived in poverty for an extended time and whose efforts at improving their situation have failed to make anything better. But let us recall that everyone is unique. People living in the best environments can naturally skew toward negative time perspectives. At the same time, people living in abject poverty can naturally skew toward positive time perspectives. Time perspective research indicates that, depending on personality and upbringing, impoverished people might lean toward a present hedonistic mindset—living from moment to moment, seeking pleasure to replace feelings of despair. Or they could have a present fatalistic frame of mind, having lost hope of achieving better conditions. A present fatalistic mindset is also understandable for those who have or believe they have an incurable illness. (As an aside, people with post-traumatic stress often concede control of their lives in this way.)

A Third Path: The Expanded Present

We'd like to share with you a third point of view about the present that is very different from present fatalism and present hedonism. If a person lives in this time perspective, they don't need therapy because they are already living in balance. The *expanded present* is the absolute present, a concept central to Buddhism and meditation. It's very different from the Western linear view of time. In the absolute present, both the past and the future are considered. The present is neither tied to the past nor a way to the future. Daily meditation gives the practitioner the experience of being in the present moment, unfiltered through the lenses of the past or the future.

In the expanded present, you open your mind fully to the present moment and release yearning and desire for future possibilities as you surrender past regrets and commitments. This form of present attention, or mindfulness, can fill your entire being, replacing your sense of past and future with a feeling of everything being one. With this perspective, the past, the present, the future, the physical, the mental, and the spiritual elements in life are not separate but closely interconnected within you. The expanded present reflects neither the pleasure seeking of present hedonism nor the cynicism and resignation of present fatalism.

In Sanskrit, India's classical language, there is an ancient saying by the philosopher-poet Kalidasa that captures this particular point of view:

> Yesterday is already a dream
> And tomorrow but a vision
> But today well lived makes every yesterday a dream of
>   happiness
> And every tomorrow a vision of hope.

Although the expanded present is not common in Western thinking, "mindfulness" as a form of meditation is becoming increasingly popular. Many Western philosophers and theologians have written about the expanded present as something of an idea. The present contains the reconstruction of time that has passed and the construction of virtual time that will soon be present. The past and future are abstractions, mental constructions that are subject to distortion, wishful thinking, and the psychological disorders of depression, anxiety, and worry.

We note that this Buddhist belief is similar to the spiritual root of many Indigenous cultures around the world, which is that all things, physical and spiritual, are connected.

The expanded present is a healthy perspective to have!

Noelle's Journey from Present Fatalism to Present Hedonism

Remember Noelle from Chapter Two? Let's check back in with her to see how she was able to turn her present fatalistic mindset into a healthy present hedonistic time perspective. We'll start with Noelle in her own words, followed by her TP therapist's thoughts.

I had learned to replace my negative thoughts about the past with positive experiences I had with Brian and my kids. There were so many; it became easy to do. But I still felt like I didn't deserve to enjoy myself. If Brian couldn't experience things with me, then I didn't want to make memories without him. The TP therapist made me promise to make short day trips on the weekends. I think she was in cahoots with my daughter Lily, who had been to see her (the TP therapist), because I didn't really feel like doing it. Sometimes it took a lot of convincing for me to go. But I always did. Part of me thought Lily needed it more than me!

Sometimes we'd go for a long, scenic drive. Other times we'd park the car and take a walk on a country road or in the forest, or we'd go to the aquarium, or the winery, or window shopping. It felt good to get out in nature and to be with people, too. Maybe we both needed this special time together to get reacquainted and make new memories.

Then, one day at the end of a TP session, a strange thing happened: It was as if something clicked in my head, and I started noticing the paintings in the therapist's office. I asked whether they were new. She told me they had been there the whole time, but I hadn't been aware of them! When she walked me to my car, like she always did, I started seeing the flowers in the trees and noticing how blue the sky was. I could hear the birds singing. It was like I had suddenly awakened from a long, dark sleep.

· · ·

Since her husband's passing, Noelle's grieving process overlapped with her PTS symptoms, causing her to experience survivor guilt. She would not allow herself to feel joy or happiness, believing she did not deserve to feel these emotions without her husband.

Note: Having treated clients with severe PTS, including seasoned war veterans, the TP therapist was familiar with this way of thinking, which can be a PTS symptom known as "survivor guilt." Survivor guilt (also known as survivor syndrome) occurs when a person feels in some way to blame for surviving a traumatic experience when others died. It can also occur when a person believes they could have done more to save the lives of others or when another person died saving them.

While in session with Noelle, the therapist was reminded of an Afghanistan war veteran she had worked with who lost his best friend during a heavy firefight with Taliban fighters. Since his return to civilian life, the veteran lived in present fatalism and suffered survivor guilt. After a series of TP therapy sessions focused on boosting past positives and selected present hedonism, he decided that instead of constantly feeling sad and guilty about the loss of his friend, he would live life "double." In other words, he would live his life as well as the life his buddy would never have a chance to experience. In this way, he would honor his friend. He increased his present hedonism by taking time to enjoy whatever he was doing and paying extra attention to all the good things life had to offer him. He also found fulfillment in socializing with fellow veterans and helping older vets with household repairs in his spare time.

Using this template, the TP therapist focused on ways to improve Noelle's present hedonistic time perspective and lessen her present fatalistic thoughts and behaviors. To boost her present hedonism and ensure that she wasn't isolating at home (present fatalism), each weekend, along with the help of her daughter, Noelle would create opportunities to experience joy. At their next session, Noelle would share with the therapist what adventure she had experienced. This proved to be a successful formula, as Noelle conveyed that she and her daughter took great pleasure not only in the activities they chose but also in how they grew closer.

As an aside, after a breakthrough session in which Noelle realized she was not to blame for her husband's death, she experienced a significant shift in her way of thinking, as evidenced by her ability to once again notice and appreciate her surroundings.

Let's Get Started

The first step we take is realizing that life is different now—perhaps more different than we could have ever imagined. This doesn't have to be a bad thing, especially when we take the next step, which is realizing that we have choices. We can choose to live in present fatalism or not, because present fatalism is, to a large degree, a mindset. We can help ourselves climb out of present fatalism by exploring present hedonism and learning to enjoy ourselves once again in the moment. By doing this, we automatically lower present fatalism. And when we are conscious in the moment when something that makes us feel good is happening, we are creating what will become past positives that can be drawn on in the future.

As a point of interest, ZTPI research indicates that most men score fairly high in present hedonism. So do teenagers and most women without children. Meanwhile, women with children tend to score high in the future time perspective, as they must plan ahead for their offspring. But we believe with the increasing number of young men taking on more responsibility in households and childrearing, future research will find they, too, will score higher in future orientation.

Some grieving people (especially those also suffering from PTS) with high past negative/low past positive and high present hedonism scores might be sublimating their symptoms in unhealthy ways through addiction (alcohol, drugs, food, etc.). This is present hedonism in the extreme. We all know that a person can overcome addiction only if they want and choose to do so. If this is what you or a loved one is experiencing (unless they are terminally ill), please see an expert for help. Once you are on the road to recovery, return to TPT to assist you in coping with both grief and PTS.

The series of exercises we are suggesting focuses on improving the way we see ourselves and then making positive choices in order to boost *selected present hedonism* and tamp down present fatalistic thoughts and actions. Selected present hedonism is using present hedonism in a healthy way, such as doing something fun or enjoyable as a reward for an accomplishment of some sort (for instance, completing a task). It's a little like how some parents reward their children for completing their chores or getting good grades in school by going to the park or a film. In our case, we'll have opportunities to make good, healthy choices and be good parents to ourselves. We'll start with some exercises that can help improve our psychological health by increasing our self-compassion.

Taking a cue from the expanded present (see "A Third Path: The Expanded Present" earlier in this chapter), being present means that instead of focusing on what happened yesterday or what could happen tomorrow, you are simply here, now. It's about getting off autopilot and becoming aware of the automatic actions and reactions you are used to and finding a place of clarity and calm. The present moment can offer us peace.

Be Kind to Yourself

Expressions of grief—those heightened emotions, like deep sadness or intense anxiety—do not define who we were, are, or will be. An important step in the course of our healing is when we realize we're temporarily off-kilter, that our normal behavior has changed during the grieving process, and it's tied to how our life used to be. When we're aware that grief is affecting us, we can stop chastising ourselves for not handling things as well as we used to or will again in the future.

Digging a little deeper, people who are grieving can experience symptoms similar to post-traumatic stress, like sleep deprivation or insomnia, difficulty concentrating, and irritability. When this happens, we can overreact to situations that might not have bothered us before the loss. By examining our present fatalistic thoughts, we might realize that we may have misunderstood someone or a circumstance while we are mourning. As we work on being more compassionate to ourselves, we can use our discernment and decide whether it's appropriate to explain ourselves or our actions to others. Besides mending fences, this process can help those who care about us to better understand and know how to be there for us during this challenging time.

When you're up to it, try a couple or all four of these simple exercises. If you aren't into writing, then please do try 1, 2, and/or 3.

1. *Self-talk*: The next time you find yourself beating yourself up for handling a situation poorly, stop the beating and take a moment to do a little positive self-talk. Tell yourself, "This, too, shall pass," or "I've been through a lot," or "I need to be compassionate with myself." We don't want to use what we're going through as an excuse for being rude or mean, especially if we were like that *before* our loss (see #2). But a little positive self-talk when we know it's necessary can go a long way toward making us feel better.

2. *Self-reflection*: Think of two recent experiences you feel you didn't handle as well as you would have liked. Perhaps you spoke disparagingly to someone who was trying to be helpful. Or you declined a phone call from a family member or friend. Is it possible your reaction was a symptom of your grief? If you believe it was, then consider how you would have handled the situation prior to your loss and whether the outcome would have been better. Likewise, if you don't think your handling of the situation was due to grief, then maybe it's time to change the way you react. When we are aware of how grief affects us and the way we behave, we can begin to heal ourselves, as well as the relationships we may have inadvertently damaged due to our grief symptoms.

3. *Positive effects*: Take a moment to touch base with your better self. Reflect on a situation in which you had a positive effect on someone else, whether someone you know or a total stranger. What was

the positive influence you had on this person? Now that you have this situation in mind, turn it around and imagine *you* were the person to receive your kindness. What was it like to be that person? Now consider being just as helpful (or even more helpful) to others in the future.

Unfortunately, most of us waste a lot of time thinking about our negative traits and don't acknowledge our virtues. Accepting our imperfections and going easy on ourselves is a big step toward improving our health. We increase our resilience when we are self-compassionate and learn from our mistakes. Then we can be open to trying again, instead of feeling guilty or ashamed that we blundered.

People who are self-compassionate feel more secure, are less likely to be depressed and anxious, and are more likely to be optimistic and happy. They are also more proactive and conscientious than those who are not self-compassionate. In addition, we boost our self-esteem as well as our resourcefulness and optimism when we view our positive actions from someone else's point of view. When we are kind to ourselves, we feel more connected to people and take better care of ourselves and others.

• • •

4. *Expressive writing*: Nobody chooses to go through the mourning process. However, strange as it may seem, sometimes grief can actually make us into better, more compassionate people. For example, some grieving people report feeling stronger because they survived their traumatic experience. Is it possible that after the loss of your loved one, you may be or are becoming a little stronger and more resilient? Do you better understand others who have gone through similar experiences? Do you have a greater appreciation for life? Take a few minutes to jot down some of the benefits you may have gained during this trying time. Perhaps you are feeling more compassionate or have reunited with family and friends. If this task is too hard, write about your positive personal qualities. Be generous with yourself.

The practice of taking a few minutes each day to write about your feelings related to an experience and thinking about the positive things that may have come out of a negative experience has beneficial psychological effects. It can reduce stress, lower blood pressure, and lead to long-term improvements in mood. When we engage in "benefit finding" (the process of acquiring positive growth from our hardships), we are more likely to be less negative, have fewer troublesome thoughts, and find more meaning in our lives.

Be Here Now

It's time we practice a little present hedonism and experience some joy. Loss and grief can cause us to feel fatalistic in the present. But by being aware of when we start to feel this way, especially when fatalism begins to drag us down, we can take action and reverse these depressing feelings and thoughts. When we replace present fatalism with selected present hedonism, we improve the way we view life and also help balance our time perspectives.

Try these simple exercises to practice living in and enjoying the present:

1. *Focus.* Wherever you are right now, focus on something in your environment that makes you feel good. It can be anything, even an aspect of something—like the way an object feels or smells or sounds. It could be a color or the way something tastes. When we notice our surroundings, or are "mindful" of the things around us, we are activating our brain. When this happens, we strengthen our positivity and have a better chance of being happier in the future.

2. *Change it up.* When you're feeling down, help yourself get out of the funk by changing up your environment. All it takes is a couple of minutes. Just going into another room can change your perspective. Of course, if you can step outside for a little bit—or even *look* outside— that would be great. Find something in your "new" surroundings that you appreciate. It could be a throw pillow, or some books, or a tree, or birds or the color of the sky.

3. *Take a break.* Do something *you* find enjoyable soon, like today— or tomorrow. It could be by yourself, like rereading a book or watching a film you previously enjoyed. Or you could invite a family member or friend to take a walk through the neighborhood, or join you for a meal, or visit the park. Whatever you choose to do, notice that when you look around, there are lots of things to appreciate in your life.

It's easy to get stuck in negativity when we're mourning. Sometimes it's like everything has a dark tint because we're wearing sunglasses all the time, and we don't need to. So when we take off the "sunglasses" and notice the beauty in our environment, we're letting the light in, which automatically increases our sense of well-being. We also enhance our peace of mind and our positivity. As simple as it may seem, all of this helps pave the way for a more favorable view of our life and our future.

Reconnect

As we know, depression is a part of the grieving process, and avoidance and isolation are symptoms of depression. It's normal for grieving people to sometimes avoid places, things, and individuals or groups that remind them of their loss. Unfortunately, this practice can lead to avoiding almost everyone and everything. Then our relationships suffer. Wanting to be alone is understandable when we're mourning. It's an important facet of grief and is necessary for us to work through our thoughts and feelings. But we can also slip into unintended isolation. It might start by simply wanting to be alone for a few days and then slowly escalate to taking meals by ourselves, putting people off, or not showing up when we say we will.

Our post-trauma research indicates that being around and engaging in activities with others (that is, being prosocial) is vital to overcoming avoidance and isolation. It helps us realize that the present has many good things to offer and people with whom to connect. When we isolate ourselves, we miss out on new experiences we could be having. More important, we're excluding our friends and family, those crucial relationships we used to have prior to our loss.

If you've been isolating—and even if you haven't—consider these tips to help you reconnect with others:

1. *Connect.* Choose someone you're close to, or someone you haven't been in contact with in a while, and connect with them. This can be over the phone or, if that's too much of a leap, via email or messaging. The goal is to have a meaningful conversation, or back and forth, to catch up. Afterward, reflect on how it felt to be in contact with this person. Then consider reaching out in this way two or three times a week to other people you haven't been in touch with lately. Remember, they may be waiting to hear from you, not wanting to intrude or push you before you're ready.

2. *Let's meet up.* Invite someone you enjoy being with to do something with you. This person might also be affected by the loss that you experienced. Or you can choose someone who is not affected by your loss. Whatever you do—whether it is an activity you're used to or something totally new—the point is that you are sharing an experience together. This one-on-one contact is what's important. Of course, you can invite more than one person to join you if you're up to it. Taking a walk in nature, meeting up for a meal, going to a movie—these things

allow you to focus on something other than your grief while you're reconnecting with people. When you're together, you may notice that your friend or relative might be trying to cope with their own grief or other issues and that you're not alone in dealing with your own pain. And you might even be able to help them, or maybe just connecting will help you both.

When we have an increased sense of belonging and we feel like we're part of a community, then depression and the negative thoughts and actions associated with grief are reduced. People who have shown signs of isolation and withdrawal due to post-trauma (to which grief symptoms are similar) display improvement—better relationships with family and fewer mood disturbances—when they participate in activities with others. The human-to-human connection is a wonderful gift we should enjoy in the present. So let's focus on building and maintaining healthy family relationships, friendships, and participating in prosocial activities.

Note: If you now have a disability and can no longer do what you used to enjoy, then now is a good time to discover new things that will bring you joy. These can be simple things, like sitting in the sun, listening to music, playing board games with family, or visiting a flower shop. Also, taking care of something living can help lift depression and make us feel connected. If you don't have a pet, explore the possibility of getting a small dog or cat. Or grow a little, easy-to-tend garden; many herbs and plants can be grown indoors.

Flip the Switch and Then Go Random

Experiencing negative thoughts and overthinking issues and situations is normal for most of us sometimes, but it can be a real problem when we're mourning. We might think we're figuring things out or working on what's troubling us when we overanalyze. But when we overthink, we can become anxious, and then we only add to the problem. When this happens, it helps to realize what we're doing as soon as possible and switch our focus to something positive. Here are a few suggestions for what to do when this happens; if you aren't into writing, then try tips 1 and 3:

1. *Switch.* When you find yourself feeling sad or having murky thoughts—in other words, you're feeling present fatalistic—switch your focus to something beautiful or wonderful in your surroundings. Maybe it's a vase of flowers on the table, or the smell of coffee from your

mug, or the sound of birds singing in the distance. This super-quick mini-mind-vacation can break the cycle and give you the opportunity to reset your way of thinking.

2. *Pick up your pen.* Try shifting your focus from what's going on in your head to what's happening around you. Then write a list of positive things about yourself, your life, your past, and your present. By taking the time to change your perspective in this way, you may find more positive things about yourself and your life than when you are in your head, overthinking.

3. *Go random.* By this, we mean practice random acts of kindness. We all have positive energy inside us, and there's no time like the present to start practicing being kind to others. Here are a few ideas to help you get started:

- Give an honest compliment to someone—this could be to someone you know or a stranger like the person passing you as they walk their dog. The compliment could be something like "That casserole you made me was delicious," or "Your dog is so well behaved." No matter what your compliment is, make sure you say it sincerely. Otherwise, it doesn't count.
- Help an elderly person get an item off a shelf at the grocery store. He or she will think you are their hero.
- Donate old books or clothes to a charity.
- Slip positive messages into books at the library.
- Drop lucky pennies (heads up!) on the sidewalk for people to find.
- Bake cookies for your neighbors.

Switching our focus from present fatalism to present hedonism is as easy as turning our head, searching for something we enjoy or find beautiful in our environment and appreciating it for a few moments. This process might sound *too* easy, but when we continue to practice this simple technique, and make it a habit, there's a good chance we'll transform our negative mindset to a positive one. Bonus: When we add the acts of doing kind things for others, we further reduce our anxiety and stress.

To Sum Up

- As our aging population continues to increase, a growing number of people who aren't health care professionals are providing care for others. It's likely that in a lifetime, one in three people will be a caregiver.

- Caregiver stress is the emotional and physical stress of caregiving. Some symptoms of caregiver stress are feeling overwhelmed or constantly worried, feeling tired often, becoming easily irritated or angry, loss of interest in activities you once enjoyed, sadness, frequent headaches, and bodily pain or other physical problems.
- A few tips to help manage caregiver stress: accept and seek help, set realistic goals for what you can and cannot do, be social, establish personal health goals, set a good sleep routine, keep up with your doctor appointments.
- Hospice focuses on care, comfort, and quality of life for a person with a terminal illness; it also provides support for the family. Although all attempts to cure are ended, other medical care continues as long as it is helpful.
- Some family members of the person who has passed on might display greed for the material and financial goods of the deceased. This conduct is generally due to narcissism and feelings of entitlement. It can lead to familial estrangement.
- By making your wishes clear through a living will and a last will and testament, you are helping those you leave behind.
- Present hedonists live for the moment; they are pleasure seekers and make decisions based on "now." Children, teenagers and some young adults are generally biased toward present hedonism due to lack of life experience. However, too much present hedonism can lead to addiction (alcohol, drugs, food, gambling, internet, sex, shopping, video games).
- When grieving, it's possible to have a *temporary present fatalistic* mindset due to current circumstances. If this is the case, it is situational.
- True *present fatalists* may believe that everything is determined by fate, by external forces, or by religiously determined destiny. They don't see much value in planning and considering behavioral options because they believe the outcome of each decision or problem is predetermined.
- The *expanded present* is a concept central to Buddhism and meditation. It is similar to the spiritual root of many worldwide Indigenous cultures, which is that all things, physical and spiritual, are connected.
- By exploring selected present hedonism and relearning to enjoy ourselves in the moment, we automatically lower present fatalism.

Bonus: We're also creating what will become past positives that can be drawn on in the future.

- People who are self-compassionate feel more secure, are less likely to be depressed and anxious, and are more likely to be optimistic and happy. Further, when we are kind to ourselves, we feel more connected to people and take better care of ourselves and others.
- The practice of expressive writing and "benefit finding" can reduce stress, lower blood pressure, help produce long-term improvements in mood, and help us find more meaning in our lives.
- When we find ourselves slipping into present fatalism, taking a break—for instance, changing our environment by walking into another room, or focusing on something in our surroundings that brings us joy, or taking a brief walk outside—can quickly improve our mood.
- People who have shown signs of isolation and withdrawal due to post-trauma (to which grief symptoms are similar) display improvement—better relationships with family and fewer mood disturbances—when they participate in activities with others.
- Overthinking can make us anxious. When this happens, it helps to realize what we're doing as soon as possible and switch our focus to something positive or beautiful in our environment. In this way, we can reset how we're thinking. When we add to this the act of doing kind things for others, we further reduce our anxiety.

REFERENCES

ACS Staff. (2019, May 10). What is hospice care? *American Cancer Society*. https://www.cancer.org/treatment/end-of-life-care/hospice-care/what-is-hospice-care.html.

Biddle, M. (2015, March 4). Men tend to be more narcissistic than women, study finds. *Science Daily*. https://www.sciencedaily.com/releases/2015/03/150304104040.htm.

Chapman, F. (2022, June 7). How narcissism can lead to sibling estrangement. *Psychology Today*. https://www.psychologytoday.com/us/blog/brothers-sisters-strangers/202206/-how-narcissism-can-lead-to-sibling-estrangement.

Grijalva, E., Newman, D.A., Tay, L., Donnellan, M.B., Harms, P.D., Robins, R.W., & Yan, T. (2015. March). Gender differences in narcissism: A meta-analytic review. *Psychological Bulletin, 141*(2), 261–310.

Henrickson, H. (2015, September 30). Toxic habits: Overthinking. *Scientific American*. https://www.scientificamerican.com/article/toxic-habits-overthinking1/.

History.com Editors. (n.d.). Hinduism. https://www.history.com/topics/religion/hinduism#.

History.com Editors. (n.d.). Islam. https://www.history.com/topics/religion/islam#.

History.com Editors. (n.d.). Judaism. https://www.history.com/topics/religion/judaism.

Hölzel, B.K., Carmody, J., Vangel, M., Congelton, C., Yerramsetti, S.M., Gard, T., & Lazar, S.W. (2011, January 30). Mindfulness practice leads to increases in regional brain gray matter density. *Psychiatry Research, 191*(1), 36–43.

Three: The Present

Kilpatrick, L.A., Suyenobu, B.Y., Smith, S.R., Bueller, J.A., Goodman, T., Creswell, J.D., Tillisch, K., Mayer, E.A., & Naliboff, B.D. (2011, May 1). Impact of mindfulness-based stress reduction training on intrinsic brain connectivity. *NeuroImage, 56*(1), 290–98.

Mayo Clinic Staff. (2023, April 6). Narcissistic personality disorder. *Mayo Clinic.* https://www.mayoclinic.org/diseases-conditions/narcissistic-personality-disorder/diagnosis-treatment/drc-20366690,

Mayo Clinic Staff. (2023, August 9). Caregiver stress. Mayo Clinic. https://www.mayoclinic.org/healthy-lifestyle/stress-management/in-depth/caregiver-stress/art-20044784.

National Institute on Aging Staff. (2021, May 14). What are palliative care and hospice care? *National Institute of Health.* https://www.nia.nih.gov/health/what-are-palliative-care-and-hospice-care.

Newsweek Staff. (2003, November 23). After the funeral, the vultures descended. *Newsweek.* https://www.newsweek.com/after-funeral-vultures-descended-133573.

Oxford English Dictionary. Oxford, UK: Oxford University Press.

Pennebaker, J.W., & Chung, C.K. (2014). Expressive writing: Connections to mental and physical health. In H.S. Friedman (Ed.), *The Oxford handbook of health psychology.* Oxford, UK: Oxford University Press.

Peterson, Chris. (2006). *A primer in positive psychology.* Oxford, UK: Oxford University Press.

Seaburn, David. (2016, October 11). How long does the present last? *Psychology Today.* https://www.psychologytoday.com/us/blog/going-out-not-knowing/201610/how-long-does-the-present-last#.

Synergy Wellness Staff. (n.d.). Most common types of addiction. *Synergy Wellness.* https://synergywellnesscenter.com/blog/the-most-common-types-of-addiction/.

Zimbardo, P., & Sword, R.K.M. (2017). *Living and loving better: Healing from the past, embracing the present, creating an ideal future with time perspective therapy.* Jefferson, NC: McFarland.

Zimbardo, P., & Sword, R.K.M. (2017). Unbridled and extreme present hedonism. In B. Lee (Ed.), *The danger case of Donald Trump: 27 psychiatrists and mental health experts assess a president.* New York, NY: St. Martin's Press.

Zimbardo, P., Sword, R.M., & Sword, R.K.M. (2012). *The time cure.* San Francisco, CA: Wiley.

And, just at the moment
when someone says, "There, she is gone,"
there are other eyes watching her coming,
and other voices
ready to take up the glad shout,
"Here she comes!"

—Henry Van Dyke

FOUR

The Future

Here we are in our final chapter: "The Future." It's hard for many of us to conceive of a future beyond a few weeks, months, or years. But others have thought far ahead for us and shared their visions of what may lie ahead. Sometimes their visions may be a little too easy for us to embrace. Depending on our generation, when we think of "The Future," our thoughts might go far ahead—like the distant future—where they may be influenced by whether we are naturally positive or negative in nature. For instance, we could go dark and think of *1984*, *Blade Runner*, *The Hunger Games* or *Dune* when we try to envision the future. By contrast, if we are the type of person who thinks more positively, we might think of *The Jetsons*, *Star Trek*, or, arguably, *Interstellar*. But for our purposes, let's set thoughts of the distant future aside and focus on *our* brighter—but different—futures.

Dr. Summer Allen is a research/writing fellow with Greater Good Science Center in Berkeley, California. In a 2019 article published in *Greater Good Magazine*, Allen informs us that scientists call thinking about the future "prospection," and, similar to miners prospecting for gold, prospection can help enrich our lives in at least four ways:

1. *Helps us make wiser decisions*: Thinking about our future helps us decide how to act now, which then affects our future.

2. *Motivates us to achieve our goals*: Thinking (not so much fantasizing) about the future can motivate us to take the necessary steps to reach our goals, but we must take obstacles into account. When we are optimistic about achieving our goals, there's a good chance we will increase our ability to achieve our goals.

3. *Improves our psychological well-being*: Overall, it appears that prospection can improve our psychological health. Thinking about the future even helps people recovering from trauma and struggling with depression.

4. *Makes us kinder and more generous*: This is a wonderful bonus

because how we think about the future can influence not only our lives but also how we treat other people. For instance, if we can picture ourselves helping people, or someone specific in the future, we are much more likely to actually do so.

So let's get started being our future-oriented "better selves"! We'll begin with a topic that we frequently take for granted: the environment and, more specifically, nature.

The Importance of Nature

Birth is followed by life, and then the inevitable: death. Is there anything more natural than this progression? Perhaps not. We are all part of nature, and we are all familiar with the natural cycle of life, as demonstrated in the seasons. Birth and blooming in the spring is followed by growth and maturation in the summer, fruition in the fall, and death in the winter. And then the cycle starts over again with renewed hope and birth in the next spring. Each one of us, in our own unique way, is a perfect reflection of the life cycle—and nature.

In recent years, an increasing body of research has pointed to the many beneficial effects that spending time in the natural world has on our health. What we've discovered is that walking or being in a natural environment—as opposed to being in an urban area—reduces stress, anxiety, and depression, and it even promotes the healing process. Further, if you can't be outdoors in nature, simply looking at a natural environment can still improve your health.

Mother Nature

Like a good parent, nature accepts us for who we are. When we're mourning, there can be so much expected of us—so many things to do; so many people to tend to; so much responsibility. Grief can be exhausting. Until now, we may not have realized that there is a place we can go to disconnect from the chaos. A place that is waiting with open arms, ready to embrace us and help soothe our minds. A place where we can give our brains a reprieve or better process all that is going on, if need be. A place to feel rejuvenated, even if only for a little while. Where? In nature. Moreover, nature can help reconnect us to the wonder and beauty that surrounds us.

Two Hours a Week

Recently, social psychologist Dr. Mathew White and his team at the European Centre for Environmental & Human Health at the University of Exeter conducted a study of 20,000 individuals. They found that when people spent two hours a week in green settings, such as parks or other natural environments—either all at once or spaced over several visits—they were much more likely to report feelings of good health and believe that their psychological well-being had improved. The results spanned across ethnic groups, various occupations, socioeconomic brackets, and levels of health. Being in nature can also lower blood pressure, stress hormone levels, nervous system arousal, and anxiety. In addition, your self-esteem and mood are enhanced by being in nature.

Bringing Nature to You

Not everyone has the opportunity to immerse themselves in an outdoor natural environment. But there are ways to bring nature into *your* environment that are easy—and helpful for mental health. Perhaps you may be doing these things already. Growing living plants and flowers—or tending to a potted herb garden—is a great option. Pets (which are also of nature) likewise keep us connected to the natural world. Taking the time to notice and appreciate trees, flowers, and greenery, even when we live in cities, can help calm our minds and soothe our souls.

Connecting with Something Greater Than Ourselves

Some people have shared that, instead of being in structures built for worship, they feel closer to God in a natural environment where they can freely express their joy and gratitude. This is understandable since we are born of nature. We live on Planet Earth. And when we die, our bodies return to the earth. No matter our religious beliefs—if we have any—nature is an all-encompassing force that envelops all of us. It is as if we innately know, deep inside us, that when we are surrounded by a natural environment, we open our minds to experiencing something pure, something rejuvenating, something nurturing—and perhaps something greater than ourselves.

• • •

Here are a few suggestions for you to consider from seasoned grief counselor Claire Willis and her coauthor Marnie Crawford Samuelson (both based in Massachusetts):

Sit quietly for a few moments, resting in the feeling and flow of your breathing, in and out. Say slowly, to yourself, the following phrases:

May I allow nature to restore my spirit.
May I find comfort in the presence of animals.
May I notice rhythms of death and renewal all around me.

Spend some time in nature:

- Using *all your senses*, notice what's around you.
- Listen to whatever sounds arise and fade, feel the breeze on your skin, or smell fresh grass or decaying leaves.
- Dwell on these sensations for a few minutes.
- Look for something in the natural world that seems to reflect your grief.
- Consider nature's cycle: life, death, decay, rebirth, restoration, and rejuvenation.
- Can you sense nature's transforming power?

Spend some time with animals:

- Go for a walk with a dog or volunteer at an animal shelter.
- Watch and play with your cat.
- Sit outside and watch birds flying or squirrels burying acorns.

Try to spend even a few minutes in or around nature as often as possible—whether that be on your porch or in your backyard. Examining the piece of fruit in your hand before you bite into it can lighten your mood and fill your heart with appreciation for the beautiful planet we all share.

Music and Grief

For some of us, the soundtrack of our lives—the music we associate with certain people, events or experiences, seasons, or entire decades that plays along with the visuals we conjure in our minds—holds special meaning. For most of us, hearing a song or melody can immediately pull us back in time to a particular setting that includes who we were with and what we were doing.

Music, like visual arts such as paintings, films or plays, can uplift us or bring us down. It can be a soothing balm to our ears and soul or as cringingly grating as the sound of fingernails on a chalkboard. It can be a spiritual experience, or set the mood for a romantic encounter, or rile us up. Music can carry greater or lesser importance at different times in our life. But rare is the person who doesn't like music. (That's called "musical anhedonia," which is a neurological condition that affects about 5 percent of the population.)

In the past few decades, hundreds of studies on the benefits of music have strongly indicated that music reduces stress and depression and can improve the way our immune systems work. One study discovered that listening to music before surgery reduced anxiety more effectively than prescription drugs. According to Joanne Loewy, director of the Armstrong Center for Music and Medicine at Beth Israel Medical Center, "Music very much has a way of enhancing quality of life and can, in addition, promote recovery."

Music Therapy

While we aren't suggesting that you need music therapy or that it is part of TPT (it isn't), we thought, given all of the above points, it might be a good idea to share some information about this relatively new discipline. Music therapy is goal oriented and can include listening to music, discussing or making music, writing songs, singing, and even dancing. You don't need a music background to benefit from its many effects.

Here's a quick music lesson provided by Faith Halverson-Ramos, a licensed mental health therapist in Colorado with a focus on music therapy:

The elements of music … are rhythm, dynamics, melody, harmony, and tone color.

- Rhythm refers to beat, meter, tempo, and syncopation. It involves the duration of sound through time.
- Dynamics relates to how loud or how soft the music is. They can change gradually or change suddenly.
- Melody involves the linear arrangement of pitches. It is the part of the song that one usually sings or hums because it is "catchy."
- Harmony is what happens when pitches come together. It adds fullness to the music, and it is the harmony that gives a piece of music a sense of "tonal home."
- Tone Color, or timbre, are the unique sounds of instruments and their musical ranges. For example, the voice sounds different than a piano. Likewise, while their ranges overlap some, they are also different.

Music therapists utilize and modify these elements to support therapeutic change. That is because, as it turns out, our brains and bodies are designed to respond to music. It can affect our breathing, influence movement, and prompt speech, in addition to the ways music can affect us emotionally, mentally, and existentially.

SOUND THERAPY

Like music therapy, sound therapy is not part of TPT. But we thought some readers might be interested in this "new" (to the West) technique, which is different from music therapy. Kendra Cherry, a psychosocial rehabilitation specialist, psychology educator and contributor at *Very Well Mind* in New York, has researched sound therapy. She notes that although there are few scientific studies about the benefits to this type of therapy, anecdotal evidence indicates they may promote relaxation, improve sleep, reduce depression, lower blood pressure and relieve pain.

The primary instrument used in sound therapy is the Tibetan or Himalayan singing bowl. These bowls, which are made of various metals, vibrate and produce rich, deep tones. They are played by either striking the sides of the bowl with a small wooden mallet or pressing the mallet in a circular motion against the outer rim of the bowl. You can also strike the bowl with the mallet just prior to starting the circular motion.

Some massage and yoga therapists have incorporated Tibetan singing bowls into their treatment practices. But Buddhist monks have been using singing bowls in conjunction with meditation for centuries. The new meditation experience called "sound baths" incorporates the bowls to "bathe" participants in the resonant sounds.

• • •

To be clear, we aren't suggesting that you need these therapies. We simply hope to show you that science indicates listening to music or sounds—like those made by a Tibetan bowl—can be beneficial to your mental health. And when we're grieving, we can all use a little assistance. This form of help is as easy as listening to your favorite tunes. We've learned that when we're feeling especially sad or mourning, sometimes it's helpful to throw open the floodgates and start thinking of other sad things—sort of pile it on for a limited amount of time (say, ten minutes or so)—and let sorrowful feelings wash over us and get them out of our system. Listening to music that brings back sad memories can kickstart this process. Then, to get yourself out of this funk, follow up by listening to more upbeat music that makes you happy.

Rose: Facing the Future

Within a couple of months of Rick's passing, my PCP as well as a close doctor friend asked me once again whether I'd like to take an antidepressant. They were concerned about the trauma I had endured over the past year and a half as well as the stress and accompanying depression of being newly widowed. Within two weeks of Rick's passing, I had organized a memorial service with three hundred people in attendance, turned over the clinic to a trusted psychologist friend (my heart wasn't in clinical work—not without Rick), and moved households. Within five weeks of Rick's passing, I saw my youngest child off to start being a university student an ocean and a continent away on the East Coast of the United States.

Rick and I had looked forward to the day when our children would be in college or beyond. We would miss them, but we would also have more time to focus on each other, our work, TPT presentations, writing projects, and travel. Now I was a widowed empty nester with only our old dog, Hina, to keep me company. I understood the doctors were trying to help, but I didn't want to take an antidepressant. I wanted to feel the loss and grief naturally. I wanted to mourn my beloved Rick and the life we knew and had planned to enjoy together. I went from living a busy life in a bustling household full of people coming and going all the time to being quietly alone. It was extremely difficult for me.

But I gave myself permission to feel the deep sorrow—what the hospice staff called anticipated grief—I had been putting off since Rick's diagnosis. I had kept myself busy with the daily tasks and demands of caregiving and restructuring our lives during my husband's illness and the necessary business after his death, not fully allowing for the emotions I knew would hit me later, when I felt I could finally give myself over to the heartbreak of losing my darling Rick. Not wanting to burden family and friends, or relive it with them, I didn't really talk to anyone about this process. It was painful enough without sharing, and I didn't want those closest to me to worry. But I did want to feel these feelings. That was my personal choice. Grief is something we all experience at some point in life. But when it did catch up with me, it was overwhelming. About three months after Rick's passing, I realized I was diving deeper and deeper into debilitating grief and depression. For the good of myself and my children, I knew I had to start working my way back up and out of the dark pit of despair—my present fatalism. I was ready.

Using the TPT protocol Rick and I had employed for years with clients, I started with the past. I suffered from nightmares and flashbacks of Rick's physically painful experiences during his fight with cancer. Most mornings I would wake with my pillow wet from tears and my eyes crusted shut from dreams and nightmares. My subconscious was working overtime when I slept, trying to cope with and make sense of what had happened. And throughout the day I would flashback to scenes of Rick in horrible pain.

Intent on working myself up and out of despair, I devoted a couple of days to recalling wonderful experiences we had shared throughout the years. Fun times with friends. Loving times with family. Helping people together. We had lived a good life and brought out the best in each other. I took brief notes about each experience to help me remember and created my own treasure trove of past positive memories and made sure they were readily available to draw on. So, from that point forward, whenever I felt a negative flashback start to enter my mind, I opened the chest and marveled at the happy memories shining up at me. It didn't take long to make this habit of replacing past negatives with happy past positives a part of my daily ritual. Sure, I'd occasionally regress and allow myself to be swept away by a tsunami of grief. But eventually wonderful memories would flood back in, and soon I'd be ready to move forward and face whatever might come my way in a hopefully positive future.

Next, as I had been isolating myself in my new home for months, I needed to reintroduce present hedonism back into my life. I started going for drives in the country, which Rick and I had liked to do. These drives led to short hikes in the mountains and to watching an occasional film at the local theater with family members. I also reached out to old friends I had lost contact with during Rick's illness, and I enjoyed getting together with them over a meal or a walk on a country road. (As an aside, my children were sensitive to what I was going through. They were grieving too! They made me promise that I wouldn't go an entire day without communicating with a family member or three days without being social in some way. And once a week at minimum I would have a meal with at least one of them.)

I'm naturally future oriented, but in my grief and depression, all the plans Rick and I had made were distant and seemed nearly impossible to attain without him. But in his wisdom, and knowing I'd soon be alone, before he died he gave me some tasks to complete. He asked me to create some form of TPT that would be available as a self-help tool, finish the Time Cure *follow-up book we had started during his illness, and continue educating people about TPT. I gave him my word that I would.*

So I rolled up my sleeves and, within a year, with the help of one of my sons, I developed two apps based on TPT. (Because of a series of extensive and costly updates required by the host company, the apps were discontinued after a few years.) Then I focused on completing our book with Phil and simultaneously even wrote a work of fiction. Living and Loving Better *was released by McFarland in November 2017. Completing the book and publishing the apps with my dear buddy Phil's help felt like I had fulfilled two of the promises I had made to Rick. That made me feel really pleased.*

Then Forum Media Polska (a Polish-based company) as well as Happify asked Phil and me to work with them on TPT education and apps to help people overcome post-traumatic stress and grief. Along with Phil, I continue to write columns for Psychology Today *and FMP's* Psychology in Practice *journal.*

Most recently, Phil and I have been working with a trio of mental health professionals in Ukraine. Our intention is to help soldiers, veterans, and civilians learn to cope with trauma and post-traumatic stress as well as grief and loss due to the Russian invasion in their country.

I share this very personal story as an offering, that it may provide a modicum of hope for those who have yet to see the light at the end of the tunnel. What lies ahead may at first appear as an oh-so-faint glimmer, so faint you'll wonder whether it's there. But it is there, waiting for you. Trust that, and move forward toward your brighter future. Like me, you may find that it's essential to have a sense of purpose. Guess you can tell I'm happiest and most fulfilled helping people, so from this vantage point, my future looks bright and full of promise. Thank you for joining me on this journey.

When Life Feels Out of Control

It's hard for many of us to keep on an even keel when circumstances in our lives start spinning out of control. And it's especially difficult when we're in mourning. One problem can quickly add to another, and so on, until we feel weighed down and powerless. No doubt some of these things will happen because we aren't at our best right now. We're sad, we're tired, we can't focus, so we're forgetful or grumpy or can't concentrate. As soon as you notice this occurring, stop, take a deep breath, and determine whether what is happening is within your control or beyond your control.

For instance, if you forgot to get something at the store, ideally, that's an easy fix and you can go back to get it or ask someone else to do so. This situation is within your control. Or if you lost your temper and had angry words for someone who didn't deserve it, you can sincerely apologize and make amends. Conversely, if you are stuck somewhere because of a storm, or someone you are waiting for hasn't arrived when they said they would due to a delayed flight, then there's no sense getting worked up. There is nothing you can do about these situations because these things are not within your control. That said, they can still be upsetting, but we don't have to make a situation worse because we aren't in control of it.

Here are some easy things that you can do if you feel like you're at your wits' end and are having a hard time coping. A couple of them may seem familiar because they work for a variety of problems. Pro tip: The more often you practice them, the easier they become and the better you'll feel.

1. Be kindhearted to yourself and others.

- *Curtail your screen time.* When we are grieving and depressed or stressed, we can slip into spending more time in front of a screen than we used to before our loss. We might think this is a simple, mind-numbing technique, and, depending on what we're watching or doing (think playing games), it can be. But too much screen time can also be a way of avoiding living life and can make us feel worse. If you feel you are addicted to the news, consider watching or reading a couple of news shows or articles a couple of times a day. (Once a day is even better.) Although news reported later in the day is more current, it's not particularly healthy to go to sleep with disturbing thoughts fresh in your mind. So make sure you read, watch, or do something that will replace unwanted thoughts well before entering your sleep routine. If you feel you watch too much of anything else, or play too many games, start self-policing your screen time. Set a timer, and then get up and walk around, do some stretching exercises, do the chore you've been putting off, call or message that person you've been ignoring, work on a project or hobby, or make plans for the following day or week. The goal is to break the cycle with an action.
- *Take mini-breaks.* We've mentioned this tip in an exercise in a previous chapter, but it's worth a reminder. These mini-breaks can be anywhere from 30 seconds to a couple of minutes, two or three times a day. Shift your focus from whatever you are doing to something that brings you a feeling of happiness. For instance, look at the flowers on the table, or the clouds floating by, or photos of loved ones, or close your eyes and go to your happy place in your mind's treasure chest. Doing so will make you feel refreshed.
- *Practice random acts of kindness every day.* Go ahead and help an elder across the street or hold the elevator door open for all to enter or exit freely, or consider putting a cheerful note under the windshield wiper of a local car with a short, upbeat message, such as "Hope you have a wonderful day!" Getting ourselves out of our heads and into positive action is a great way to fight depression. And remember: Kindness begets hopeful feelings.

2. Treat each day and every tomorrow as gifts.

- *Express love tangibly.* We all need hugs, whether they be physical or figurative, and especially when we're grieving. But instead of waiting for them to come our way, be the instigator; go ahead and be generous with hugs for loved ones. These can be gentle physical hugs, bear hugs, or even virtual hugs over the phone, *FaceTime*, or *Zoom*. In other words, use words of affection as hugs when you can't physically be with someone you love. For instance, if your child or grandchild is on the phone, you can say, "I love you so much! I'm hugging you tightly right now!" or "If we were together, I'd give you the biggest hug!" The more we express love, the more deeply we feel it and the more hopeful we'll be.
- *Remember to revel in the beauty around you.* There is beauty everywhere; sometimes we just have to shift our focus. Notice the color of the sky, the grain in the wood, the water dripping off the roof, the sound of children laughing, or bird song. Beauty is plentiful and always present. Realizing there is beauty around you helps bring it *into* you and enhances your feelings of hope.
- *Be grateful for everything.* The roof over our heads, food in the refrigerator, the warmth of a sweater, and the people in our lives, especially family and friends—all are precious. When we're grieving, it's easy to forget all the good people and things in our lives. Even in the bleakest of times, we have so much to be grateful for. Remember that lesson.

• • •

Religions and Spiritual Practices: How We Mourn—Part 4

According to the United Nations, there are over 476 million Indigenous people living in ninety countries across the globe. Of those, there are more than 5,000 distinct groups with an estimated 7,000 languages. The largest ethnicities originate in Africa, the Americas, Australia and Polynesia. Due to the thousands of people in each of these thousands of groups, there are a myriad of differences in the spiritual practices on each continent and throughout Polynesia. Yet there are also similarities. It's these similarities we'll focus on in this, our final segment of "Religions and Spiritual Practices: How We Mourn."

AFRICANS

From an African perspective, death is a natural transition from the visible to the invisible world. According to this spiritual ideology, the spirit, the essence of the person, is not destroyed but moves to live in the spirit ancestors' realm. There are three facets to a human being: The first is spiritual selfhood, which begins at conception, or perhaps earlier in an ancestral spirit that reincarnates. The second is a social or experiential selfhood, which begins at conception and continues through the introduction of the child into the human community, ending with death. Third, there is an ancestral selfhood that follows biological death. These selfhoods are interdependent and interrelated, coexisting in a collaborative and collective way. Great significance is placed on the contribution that the self—the person—makes to the well-being of others and the environment. When people die, they transcend to the spirit world to be in the company of the living dead or ancestors. Ancestors protect and provide guidance to those in the material realm and therefore are highly respected, venerated and very important to the community of the living.

The grieving process is characterized by rituals such as the bereaved family members shaving their hair and slaughtering a domestic animal. Different rituals are performed depending on who the deceased is and how they died. Practices vary among different ethnic groups, and all have symbolic significance. The performance of these rituals is seen as important in maintaining balance and harmony between the living and the living dead, who are now ancestors.

AUSTRALIAN INDIGENOUS PEOPLE

For Aboriginal people, spiritual values include a holistic sense of oneness, interdependence, reverence for land, and responsibility for others. Funeral and mourning rituals are referred to as "Sorry Business." The tradition of not depicting the deceased in print or photos or voicing their first names is very old, the belief being that in doing so, you would recall and disturb their spirit. Today, naming protocols differ from community to community and are often a family decision. However, this custom is still carried on in the Northern Territory, where traditional Aboriginal life is stronger and was left more intact after colonization. Cultural differences among tribes and clans mean that funeral traditions differ throughout the continent. But a common idea is that Aboriginal death rituals aim to ensure the safe passage of the spirit into the afterlife and to prevent the spirit from returning and causing mischief. Funerals are important communal events. Ceremonies can last for days and even weeks, with children being taken out of school to participate. There may be a series of ceremonies, dances and songs spread out over several days.

Traditionally, some Aboriginal groups buried their loved ones in two stages. In the first, they would leave the deceased on an elevated platform outside for several months. Then, once only the bones were left, they would take the bones and paint them with red ochre. The painted bones could then be buried, placed in a significant location in the natural landscape, or carried with the family as a token of remembrance. However, in modern Australia, people with Aboriginal heritage are more likely to opt for a standard burial or cremation, combined with elements of traditional culture and ceremonies.

AMERICAN INDIGENOUS PEOPLE

Today, there are well over one thousand different Indigenous tribes in North, Central, and South America. The death rituals and mourning practices of these Indigenous Americans vary widely according to each group's traditions, although those in North America share some recurrent beliefs. As with other Indigenous Peoples, the Americans believe that all things are connected. Another common aspect is the idea that the spirit of a person lives on after their physical death and then journeys into the afterlife, although there is no concept of heaven and hell. Some tribes believe that communication with the spirits of the dead is possible and that spirits can travel to and from the afterlife to visit the living. Reincarnation, in which the soul is reborn into a new body, is also a common belief among some tribes.

Many Native American and First Nation death rituals concentrate on providing the spirit with the things it needs to arrive safely at its destination. Other rituals focus on safely guiding the spirit to its home in the afterlife. In the past, some tribes would leave the body to naturally decompose in a tree or on a funeral platform, or they might leave an opening in the burial chamber so the spirit could escape. The natural decomposition also reflects the Native Americans' deep connection with nature and the cycle of life and death. A common ritual, such as smudging (the burning of special herbs such as sage) and smoking a special ceremonial pipe, might be incorporated into funeral rituals, led by the tribe's medicine man or spiritual leader. Like the Australian Aboriginals, the Navajo would refuse to use the name of the person for at least a year after their death, in the belief that it would be wrong to call back their spirit from the afterlife. Today Native Americans may still honor the traditional customs of their tribe, with or without elements of Christianity and other religions. Their spirituality remains a complex, multifaceted belief system, with many varied funeral customs to honor the dead.

We'd like to share some burial and mourning rituals of two Indigenous American tribes, one from the Far North and the other in South America.

Tlingit

According to the Central Council of the Tlingit and Haida Indian Tribes of Alaska, *SealaskaHeritgage.org*, and Tlingit author Diane E. Benson, the Tlingit have a tradition known as the "40 Day Party," which occurs on the fortieth day after the death. The clan (family) gathers for a meal and to remember the dead. But the major post-funeral ceremony is held one year after death. At this time, the community gathers to celebrate the deceased. Speeches are given by family members and clan leaders. Dances are performed while mourning songs are sung. The faces of the members of the host clan are marked with black paint, usually applied by a child. The clothing of the deceased is worn by a family member as a form of passing on their place in the family. A feast is enjoyed, followed by songs of love. Gifts such as dry goods and other items are given away to those in attendance. Then, after more dancing, money that has been collected is distributed to certain clan members who assisted in the ceremonies.

Amazon

Recently, when the chief of a Xingu tribe in the Amazon died of COVID-19, for the first time a photojournalist, Ueslei Marcelino of *Reuters*, was allowed to record part of the ceremony and mourning rituals. He shared that while women cried for days, the men fished in the river. Then the fish were roasted on an open fire and served on tortillas made by the women. Men paraded around the village and blew long bamboo trumpets. The spirit of the dead chief was honored and represented by a painted tree trunk. The men decorated their bodies with a paint made of charcoal, which was accented on their bodies with red dye. Colorful warriors danced and then participated in wrestling competitions. Later, after hours of weeping and lamentation, before daybreak, the spirit of the dead left the tree trunk to join his ancestors in the underworld.

POLYNESIANS

Throughout Polynesia—Hawai'i, New Zealand, Samoa, Tahiti, Tonga, and other Pacific island nations—an encompassing belief is that all things, living as well as inanimate, have a spiritual quality. This sacred energy is called *mana*, and it is the basis of Polynesian theology. Ancient Hawaiians believed (and many of Native Hawaiian descent still do) that protective ancestral spirits known as *'aumakua* watched over their families. Generally, these spirits could take the form of animals such as sharks, owls, geckos and so forth. To quote the late Dr. John Charlot, emeritus professor of Hawaiian and Polynesian religion at the University of Hawai'i, "Polynesians believe in life after death and that … the world of the living is in continual communion with that of the dead…. The Polynesian's understanding of family as a spiritual power, of deceased family members as continuing sources of love and care, of the closeness and communion of the living and the dead … are a genuine contribution to the world."

Multiday funeral events are customary for Pacific Islanders. The family gathers for feasting, singing, dancing, and remembrances of the deceased. Roasted pig as well as other traditional foods such as taro, yams, rice, and local fruits are enjoyed. The deceased is also remembered annually, usually on their birthday or Memorial Day. Once again, the family gathers and may visit the grave to clean it, after which fresh flowers are placed on the gravesite. The family then shares a meal followed by singing and storytelling.

• • •

Making Things Right

Two important things we share with those who have gone before us are: (1) we are human beings struggling to cope in a constantly changing world, and (2) we have all made mistakes. Unless they told us, we'll never know whether our loved one left this world with regrets. If they passed away unexpectedly, they might not have had the opportunity to reflect on their lives. If they had an illness that gave them the time to reflect, again, we wouldn't know unless they told us.

But *we* are alive, and we can take some time for deep reflection about our personal actions. This may be significant if we didn't have the opportunity to say everything we might have wanted to say to our loved one before they passed away—especially if we wanted to ask them for forgiveness for something we said or did that hurt them or wanted to forgive our loved one for a past transgression they committed that hurt us. Whether we are thinking of the deceased or someone living, this deep reflection is an important step to take to be our "better selves." It helps us clear the decks of negative feelings and open the door for making amends. In this way, we can leave behind our old baggage. Then we'll be lighter and better prepared for whatever our "new" future holds for us.

However, if what is shared in the following section, "Ho'oponopono," doesn't resonate with you, or is too difficult to consider doing now, put it aside and please consider trying the suggestions later or when you're feeling stronger.

· · ·

In conjunction with the spiritual practices of Indigenous Peoples, we'll delve into an effective method that Rose (who is part Native Hawaiian) and her husband Rick employed for decades when counseling individuals and families.

Hawai'i is the most ethnically and racially diverse state in the United States. Hawai'i is similar to other regions where different Native American ways of life have influenced the newer Western culture; the host culture of the Indigenous Peoples in Hawai'i, the Native Hawaiians, gently overlays all others. This effect can be seen in how non–Hawaiian peoples in the state, no matter where they are originally from, have been influenced by or adopted many Native Hawaiian ways of life. These include cooking and foods, music, sports, dance, natural medicines, and spiritual practices, as well as, for some, a specific psychological healing method. Since our clients were cross-generational and cross-cultural, we used this healing method in conjunction with TPT in our clinical practice when helping couples and families cope with difficult issues, including grief and loss. We're sharing it with you in case you'd like to make amends with your lost loved one or if you'd like a fresh start with someone else in your life.

Ho'oponopono

For centuries, when Native Hawaiians had relationship difficulties (and sometimes other problems), they used a technique known as *ho'oponopono* to course correct and *imua*—move forward. Ho'oponopono means "to make things right." It is the practice of sincere apology and true forgiveness, and it is still used today by many families. In the past few decades, it has found its way into mental health practices in the United States and around the globe. (When presenting on time perspective therapy in Warsaw, Poland, a few years ago, we spoke about ho'oponopono and were surprised when two Eastern European mental health professionals mentioned that they had studied this concept in Europe and used it in their practice in Poland.) When heartfelt, ho'oponopono rectifies and helps heal the person asking forgiveness and, sometimes, all the people involved in the process.

Perhaps the most important aspect of an Indigenous "psychological system"—one that appears to be universal—is an understanding of the relationship among mind, body, and spirit. Core beliefs are that the mind, the body, and the spirit are all connected and all things, whether living or inanimate, are interconnected. For instance, in this system, how and what you think not only affects you mentally and emotionally but also can affect your physical and spiritual well-being. In Polynesian cultures, it is believed that one's mistakes and social trespasses can cause physical illness or mental problems. We hope that after you review this process, you'll consider using it in your life, if and when there's a need.

There are four steps in the ho'oponopono process:

1. *Remorse*: This step may be very painful. It's when you realize that you have knowingly—and sometimes unknowingly—harmed someone and therefore harmed yourself. (Remember, we're all connected.) You may feel sorrowful and repentant. But now you are ready to make amends. Once this realization is fully attained, you move on to the next step.

2. *Forgiveness*: This is difficult to achieve for many, especially in person. It takes bravery and a humbled ego to seek forgiveness face to face. When asking for forgiveness, it must be genuine. Any "yeah, but's" won't cut it, as this is a sign that you may be finding ways to let yourself off the hook or lessen your part in whatever happened. If this occurs, you aren't ready. The desire for forgiveness must be sincere and come from the heart. If the person you are asking has passed on, then silently ask them for forgiveness. Do the same—silently—if the person is alive but it's impossible to ask forgiveness face to face or over the phone. Maybe the relationship is so far gone that there's no way you can communicate. But if it is possible to ask in person, over the phone, or via written communication (letter, email, messaging), the best you can do is hope they will be open to your request. If they refuse your apology and request for forgiveness, know you tried and, when you have a quiet moment, ask their soul to forgive your soul.

3. *Gratitude*: Feel appreciation for the other person and for the lessons they've helped teach you. The lessons may have been especially difficult, or appeared negative, but sometimes we grow by leaps and bounds *because* of these experiences. Whether in person or via writing,

or silently on your own, express your gratitude with a heartfelt "thank you." Your expression of gratitude may be confusing to the person you are asking to forgive you, especially if you are face to face or on the phone. They may be thrown off by your words of appreciation or think you are joking. But you are showing them that you've changed and that this is your new way of being. Feeling and expressing gratitude leads to the last step.

4. *Love*: Love is nice to express physically, if possible, with a handshake, hug, or whatever is fitting. You don't have to say the words "I love you" specifically, unless it's appropriate. If the other person is suspicious of your actions, they may not want to shake your hand. That's okay. If you're going through the process on your own, then imagine you are with the other person either shaking hands or gently hugging.

Once the process is completed, if the other person isn't receptive, give them time and know you've done your best. If they've passed on or the relationship is too far gone and you're on your own, you've done what you could and are a better person for allowing yourself to go through this challenging exercise.

A wonderful benefit of practicing ho'oponopono is its effect on the intrapersonal—in other words, you become more aware of how you affect others and the world around you. Ideally, this understanding leads to greater empathy and compassion. You bravely took the opportunity to learn from the experience and live through it. It's our choice to become a better, more enlightened person and work toward creating a healthier, kinder, more compassionate future for ourselves, our kin, and others.

. . .

Bias Toward the Future

We aren't born thinking, much less knowing about the future. Most of us can't grasp the concept of the future until sometime between the ages of three and five. Interestingly, research indicates that some people are more likely to think about the future than others. For instance, several conditions—including living in a temperate zone (where it's necessary to anticipate seasonal changes), living in a stable family or society, being Protestant or Jewish, and becoming educated—can create people who are future oriented. More often than not, future-oriented people do very well in their lives. They are less aggressive and less depressed, have more energy, take care of their health, and have better impulse control and more self-esteem.

In general, Americans are concerned with planning for the future. Unfortunately, people in mourning—similar to people with PTS who are stuck in past negative memories or present fatalistic thoughts—can lose the ability to even conceive of a hopeful future. But they must journey toward this future positive time perspective in order to re-create balance in their lives.

Future-oriented people don't pay much attention to past experiences, and they can put aside the din of the present insisting that they "do this now." Instead, they calculate the possible future consequences of current actions. If they find the expected anticipated costs are higher than the imagined gains, then they won't do it; the perceived risks are simply too great. But if the imagined gains dominate over the anticipated costs, then they'll proceed. Future-oriented people live in a world of contingencies, probabilities, and abstract mental representations of a virtual world on their horizon. They aren't tempted by immediate gratification that could rebound later (like unprotected sex that could result in a sexually transmitted disease or unplanned pregnancy). They are not easily persuaded by salespeople hustling questionable products or services, but they are able to take a well-reasoned chance on a new idea.

It's no wonder that the future orientation lends itself to problem solving and developing alternative strategies for reaching any given goal. Future-oriented people are intent on finishing what they start and getting the job done. They understand that although anything can happen at any time, they can still take steps to plan for a successful life. But they can also get *too* caught up in planning for the future. These are the people who can multitask like crazy while they complain "there's not enough time" or sacrifice their personal time for material success that will support their family financially.

We'd be remiss if we didn't mention that there is a smaller group of future-oriented people who focus on a *negative* future. These individuals envision an apocalyptic, dystopian eventuality for our nation and the world. We don't want to spend too much time on this mindset, as it isn't helpful to explore when we're in mourning. For the purposes of our grief work, we'll focus on creating a new and different brighter future.

Noelle's Journey into Her Brighter Future

It's time for our last visit with Noelle. Just when we think it couldn't get any worse for her, it does. You'll see why we asked whether we could share her story when you read this final installment. There are lessons to be learned from her strength and resolve. Let's find out how her story progresses, first in her own words and then through the eyes of her TP therapist.

There were many negative things that happened in my life shortly after Brian died. I had worked for a large corporation for thirty years. At first, we were told they were scaling down like a lot of companies were doing. And then, very quickly, they closed. On top of this development, the business that Brian and our children owned was going bankrupt. In our sessions, the TP therapist talked about turning lemons not just into lemonade but into something even better—maybe lemon meringue pie! She helped me plot and plan my future.

As my life was changing, I started to change things too. I had to look for a new job, and fortunately I got an even better one much closer to home. Now I work for a more diverse company that has a long and important history where I live. Along with some accounting, I get to do things that are more managerial and also fun things, like cataloging historic documents and helping to set up a museum. It's very exciting! And to top everything off, my kids and I saved the family business!

I repainted the farmhouse—inside and out—and rearranged the master bedroom. It had always been very dark and masculine. But now I could do whatever I liked. So I got lacy, floral bedding and lots of pillows, new curtains and pretty, colorful things for the bathroom. I gave away most of Brian's clothes and tools to friends and family and only kept some of his most cherished things. On Brian's birthday, we'd celebrate with a cake, and instead of ignoring him on holidays, I'd start off the meal by acknowledging him. After a while, my psychiatrist thought I was doing so well that he decreased my prescription medication. And now I no longer have to take them.

The part of planning for my positive future that caused me the most problems was being single. I had gone from my father's house to Brian's house. I had never dated anybody other than Brian, and I was afraid other women would consider me some kind of threat. I didn't want to be thought of as a husband stealer or a loose woman; that is so not me! But I had changed, and I wasn't so afraid anymore. So I asked a man out for coffee!

Both Brian and I have known him for thirty years. He's the only man outside of my family members I feel comfortable with. His parents had him late in life. He was an only child and had never married. I know he dated once in a while when he was younger. But his father became ill and was wheelchair bound from a pretty young age. His mother had always been frail. She couldn't take care of his father, so he took care of them both. He was such a good son! His mother and father died within a few months of each other, the way some old people do who have been together since childhood.

He's very respectful and considerate. I would see him at church and Bible study, and he would always seek me out to ask how I was doing. He never pressures me. He owns his own home and is retired. One day after church I just blurted out, "Would you like to get coffee with me?" and he said he'd love to! He doesn't need anything or want anything from me other than company. I've known him for more than half my life, and he has always been a kind and good friend. We go to church and Bible study together, to the movies and out for meals. We drive around sightseeing. I'm having so much fun!

• • •

Noelle suffered a series of personal disasters in the months following her husband's death. The TP therapist worked with her to focus on a positive future, even though things in her life were going horribly awry. Noelle was encouraged to take each situation separately and explore possible positive outcomes. She tried very hard to follow this advice and, when appropriate, would include her children in the process. Through ingenuity and finesse, she and her children saved their family business. Noelle found employment quickly with a local company closer to home, a position in which she can use her skills and also learn new things that she finds interesting.

Noelle and Brian had wanted to upgrade their farmhouse prior to Brian's death. As part of her future positive, Noelle made plans and then followed through with the improvements. She had entered the acceptance phase of grief and was ready to let go of most of her husband's material things while respectfully ensuring that they went to good homes. She had a small setback and felt guilty when she detected a new sense of freedom. This happened when she prepared to redecorate her bedroom and bathroom without having to consider someone else's opinion. She realized that while she had been married, she had deferred to her husband's tastes, and now it was okay to explore her own style.

The TP therapist explained that although Noelle's husband had passed away, their relationship could continue in an even more spiritual way. She was encouraged to acknowledge Brian on special occasions.

Noelle had been part of this special couple since age seventeen. Being a widow terrified her. In sessions, she explained that when she was in high school, an attractive family friend had been widowed and was almost immediately shunned by her fellow church members, including Noelle's mother. When the widow needed minor home repairs done, the men who would have helped her and her husband in the past no longer answered her calls. Their wives wouldn't allow it. The women parishioners would gossip about the widow, who was once their friend. They spread rumors and told others that she was scheming to take their husbands. The widow became a recluse, never remarried, and died at a fairly young age. This behavior had informed Noelle's future negative time perspective.

The TP therapist was amazed when Noelle shared that she had been having coffee once a week with a single man she and Brian had known for many years. The TP therapist encouraged Noelle's relationship with her new companion.

For about a year, Noelle continued with TP therapy monthly. When she felt confident that she had concluded this chapter in her rich life and was well into a new, exciting chapter, she agreed with the TP therapist that their time together was complete, with the condition that she was always welcome back if she felt the need to talk.

Update: Noelle and her new partner dated for about a year when they decided she would move in with him. They agreed that she should be the one to move, as the house she had shared with Brian held too many memories. Noelle left the large farmhouse—complete with a barn and outbuildings—to her children, which worked out well for their family business. After a few months of living together, Noelle and her beau married. Her children, having known this man since they were born, feel close to him. Noelle is living a very different life than she thought she ever would. She's very happy in her new, brighter future.

Let's Get Started

We start our journey toward a brighter but different future by using our imaginations to envision ourselves *in* the future. Then we'll make both short- and long-range plans to help us get there. This may seem like an overwhelming task, but you'll have a variety of exercises to choose from. Some of the items you might want to accomplish in the future will be easy, necessary, and uneventful things like cleaning the inside of the refrigerator, mowing the lawn, or paying bills. You'll also be encouraged to include things that improve your life. These could be as simple as planting a garden or as complicated as changing careers. It all depends on what you'd like to do in your bright new future.

Being future oriented is a healthy way to live, unless you're *too* future oriented. But we'll get to that in a minute. Research indicates that future-oriented people enjoy richer, more fulfilling lives. They are good problem solvers and aren't tempted by immediate gratification.

But when we're grieving, even a future-oriented person can temporarily be lost in negative time perspectives. We can find ourselves in a fatalistic present, stuck facing backward (where painful memories abound) and unable or unwilling to turn around to face our future. But, friend, we must journey toward this future positive time perspective to regain balance in our lives. It's our choice. So let's choose wisely.

And now we address the people who are *too* future oriented: Please slow down. When we think too much about the future, we can be fanatical multitaskers or, worse, workaholics. In this mindset, we're so intent on accomplishing whatever it is we need or want to achieve that we forget about the here and now, thus missing out on important life experiences. For some grieving people, getting lost in busy work, or real work, can feel like a good thing, and maybe it is, temporarily. But in the future, you may be headed for burnout, both physical and mental, as well as feelings of regret about the people and activities for which you didn't make time. We hope slowing down and taking the time to do some of the exercises in this book (revisit Chapter Three, specifically "Be Here Now" and "Reconnect") will help you gain balance and bring more joy to your life.

Our Brighter—and Different—Future

When we are self-aware—when we consciously know our emotions, motives, and desires—we have attained a milestone in our development as adult human beings. It's possibly the most important step toward generating a more positive present, along with a brighter future. And, being more self-aware, we realize that this new future may be very different from the future we had planned before our loss. Now that we are on the path to healing, let's start making plans for our new, and different, brighter future. We'll do this by exploring what our future might look like and setting realistic goals we can work toward to make that future come true.

This may sound like an impossible task because, more often than not, when we are mourning, our focus is on our past and the daily hardships we face in the present. The future may appear unclear, out of focus, or just plain negative because of our loss. Perhaps we think whatever we do won't make a difference or that it's too hard. When this happens, we hold ourselves back from living a more fulfilling life—and being our best selves. Well, prepare yourself for a big "but": We have a choice. We can be stuck in our grief and our past negative/present fatalism, OR we can choose to move forward to our new and brighter future.

Let's gently enter our future by remembering what we enjoyed in the past and then using our imaginations to "see" ourselves in the future. For maximum benefit, we suggest writing down your thoughts, as suggested in some of the previously described exercises. This way you'll remember what's important to you and what you intend to do, and you'll also be able to keep track of how you're doing in the future.

1. *Remember the fun stuff and do it!* Sometimes grieving people don't feel like they deserve to be happy after their loss. If they catch themselves smiling or laughing, they may feel guilty that they are experiencing joy. Perhaps they feel they should be sad all the time, or they may think that if they are happy, even for a moment, they are being disloyal to their loved one. If you find yourself immersed in this form of present fatalism, please realize that it doesn't serve you or anyone else. In fact, let's turn this idea around. Right now, try thinking about things that make you happy—things that are most meaningful to you and perhaps inspire you. These could be playing a sport with friends (such as pickleball, fishing, or golfing), or having a meal at your favorite diner with family, or going to a movie, attending a yoga class, bike riding, or having a long catch-up conversation with your bestie. Take a few moments to think about these things. Then write two or three of them down and include a few phrases that describe how and why they are meaningful to you. If you aren't into writing, then, with your utmost effort, do this exercise in your mind. Next, decide how you can dedicate more of your time to these happy-making pursuits as soon as possible—like this week. When we focus on meaningful things, our thinking shifts from negative to positive, and we can start living a more joyous life.

2. *Focus on the best and brightest.* Clear your mind as best you can, and then imagine yourself in your best and brightest future. This may be hard to do, but try it. Who are you with? What are you doing?

Where are you? How do you look? Jot down what your future looks like in detail. Or you can make a list. It's best to include a timeline with a few words indicating what you can do soon—today or tomorrow—to help make your brighter future your new reality. For example: One year from now, I will run/walk in a 6k race; I'll start today by walking six blocks in my neighborhood. Or three years from now, I will sell my pottery at the farmers' market; I'll check out affordable pottery classes nearby today.

Grieving can sometimes cause us to forget the important people and things that make us happy. When we take the time to remember, we can once again find joy and meaning waiting for us just ahead. Imagining a positive, bright future for ourselves can open our minds to a multitude of possibilities that can become our new reality. In this way, instead of grief directing us, we regain control of our lives.

Setting Goals

Setting and completing goals may not have been a problem prior to the loss of our loved one, especially if we set the big goals in our life together with the person we lost. But we might have difficulty now even thinking about goals. We might fear what the future may bring or be afraid of getting hurt. Or maybe we aren't even thinking about the future because we're stuck in present fatalism and can't perceive what our new future might look like because it will be so different from the future we had expected to have. Depression and fear are exhausting—physically and emotionally. Fortunately, there are ways we can change our negative thoughts and feelings into positive thoughts and actions. We can do this.

1. *Short-term goals*: When we set new goals to achieve, we can gain a sense of control and also build our self-esteem. Think about a few goals you'd like to complete in the next few days. These goals can be simple, like cleaning out some drawers or a closet, making a doctor's appointment you've been putting off, or inviting a friend on a walk in nature. Now, choose one of these goals. Just one. What will it take to make it happen? The hardest part is getting started. But you can pick up the phone and make that call. Or open that drawer or closet and begin sorting things into piles (keep/give away/toss). When you break through that first barrier, you might find yourself thinking, "This isn't

so bad." And once this goal is complete, you might be ready to tackle those other short-term goals you thought of a little while ago.

2. *Long(er)-term goals*: Think about a medium-range to long-term goal you'd like to accomplish. It can be a goal you've had in mind for some time or a brand-new goal. It can be physical or material, such as planting a vegetable garden over the summer, taking dance lessons, or buying a new car in three years. Or it could be intellectual, like reading a series of books, learning a new language, or taking an astronomy class. What will it take to achieve this goal? Planning where your garden will be and what vegetables you'd like to plant? Choosing what dance lessons you'd like to take? Saving some money each month to go toward a down payment on a new car? You get the idea. Once you visualize the steps you need to take, you can get started by placing one foot in front of the other and be on your way to making it happen.

3. *Short- to long-term goals*: This one is for writers (but even if you don't like to write, please read this anyway). Choose a short-term goal that might become a long-term goal that you'd like to accomplish. Now write about this goal and the steps it would take to make it your new reality. For our "for instance," we'll choose a goal that many might relate to, which is getting our health back on track, starting with our diet, which has gone astray since our loss. So we'd start by:

1. looking up appealing, healthy recipes in books or online,
2. getting the items we need to make these healthier meals,
3. making and eating these healthier meals,
4. taking walks on a regular basis, and
5. repeating these steps until we reach our goal weight.

For mid- to long-term goals, it will take time to achieve our objectives. But once we penetrate the barrier that has been holding us back, there may be no stopping us! We're taking control of our lives and our futures by setting and following through with our goals. Once you've started, be sure to pat yourself on the back for sticking with the plan.

Looking Forward

Right now, at this moment, we are the sum total of how we interpret all of the experiences that have happened in our lives (the negatives and the positives) as well as all that we perceive is happening to us now (more negatives and positives). So it makes sense that when we envision the future, we bring all of our, shall we say, baggage with us! This baggage includes expectations of places and, most important, people that may or may not be a fair representation of reality. When this happens, our perception of the future is influenced by what we are, maybe stubbornly, dragging behind us. The following exercises will ideally let us view our future, or possible futures, through a clearer lens.

1. *Step into the future*: Take a few moments to think of an upcoming event you are supposed to attend. This event can be in the near future or a little farther down the road. It can be big or small, and it should be something you would normally be enthusiastic about doing. For instance, it might be a film with friends, a dinner out with family, a wedding, or a hike in nature. Now imagine you are turning around 180 degrees. You are standing in the present but facing backward, looking at your past. Your past is very important. Without it, you wouldn't be the incredible person you are, but for now, you want to leave it for a bit. In your mind, give yourself a little shake and imagine you are shaking off any negativity from the past that might be attached to you.

Now imagine you are turning back around 180 degrees to face the future. Behind you is your past, and you are firmly planted in the present. The present may hold a little depression or a little negativity. We want to leave these things behind. So now imagine that you're taking a step forward with one foot. As you do this, you are leaving the present, which is also very important, but you'll be back soon enough. Now, in your mind, take a second step so that you are fully removed from the present and have stepped into the future.

You are free and clear of the past and the present, and you can now envision the upcoming event through a clear lens. Imagine yourself in the middle of it; use your senses to make the event as realistic as possible. Take your time. When you're ready, take a step back with one foot, and then the other, and you're back in the present.

Most of the time, our experiences help us make informed decisions. But sometimes our experiences can cloud what's happening now and might hold us back from doing something in the future. We can find ourselves worried or anxious. Research shows that when we anticipate an event in a good way, our optimism gets a boost. And optimistic people have good coping skills and can persevere during difficult times. It makes sense that we live happier lives when we believe good things are coming our way.

2. *Core values*: We were all raised with core values, those basic principles that guide how we behave and help us determine right from wrong. Our core values can change as we age. For example, when we are very young, our core values—those things we most cherish—might be love, family and friendship. As we age, we may add intelligence, morals, trust and tradition. (See Appendix II for a list of core values.)

Choose some core values that have been important in your life so far and then see whether there are others that you'd like to live by in the future. Use the first part of the "Step into the Future" exercise above until you are free and clear of the past and present and have stepped into the future. Now imagine your future self living with these core values. How does this make you feel? Are you living a more fulfilling life? Take your time. When you're ready and have come back to the present, take a moment to think of a way you can implement one of your new core values into your life today.

When we focus on our core values, we may find they've changed over time. For instance, before our loss, we may have prized achievement as a top core value. Maybe this mindset caused us to spend more time at work or on projects outside the home. But since our loss, we find that this core value has greatly scaled down or morphed into another core value, perhaps commitment—commitment to family, friends, and the well-being of our own self. Further, we may realize that the changes we are making, subtle though they may be, can lead to a more hopeful future.

A Good Night's Sleep Revisited

Toward the end of Chapter Two, under "A Good Night's Sleep: Deep Relaxation," we presented a technique we've shared with our clients (it's also a good technique to try with children) to help them relax into slumber. For those new to meditation, it can be an effective way to quiet your mind by focusing on your breath and your body. And since we all know the importance of getting enough sleep, which is crucial for us when our body is healing, we wanted to share a recent discovery as well as two other tried and true methods. (We note that the first exercise is a condensed version of "Deep Relaxation.")

1. *The "military method"*: Hannah Coates of *Vogue* wrote an article in 2023 about the technique known as the "military method," introduced by author and coach Lloyd Bud Winter's book, *Relax and*

Win: Championship Performance (1981). This technique is reputed
to be very effective—so effective, in fact, that Winter claims you can
fall asleep in as little as ten seconds, maximum two minutes! But to
experience the technique's full benefits, it's best to do it nightly; you
should expect good results after about six weeks of practice.

Start by lying comfortably in bed, on your back if possible, with
hands on your stomach. Now:

1. Relax your entire face, including all the muscles and your
tongue, from your jaw to inside your mouth. It can be easier to tense
them all up first and then let go.

2. Drop your shoulders to release any tension, and allow your
hands to drop to the side of your body.

3. Exhale, relaxing your chest and focusing on the breath. Also,
allow your legs, thighs, and calves to relax in the process, letting
gravity pull them down naturally.

4. Clear your mind for ten seconds, imagining a relaxing scene.
If this doesn't work, try saying the words "don't think" over and over
for ten seconds.

5. Within ten seconds, you should fall asleep, but it may take up
to two minutes, especially when you first start practicing.

Soldiers must try to sleep in peaceful as well as risky wartime conditions (and everything in between). This method was developed to help them
fall asleep quickly no matter the situation to help them minimize on-the-job
mistakes. Emphasis on alleviating muscle tension and relaxing the body
activates the parasympathetic nervous system, which is responsible for the
body's "rest and recovery" mode. If you're having a hard time falling asleep,
this method may work for you. It is like a form of self-hypnosis.

2. *Up for a bit*: If after you've practiced deep relaxation and/or the
military method twenty minutes have gone by and you're still having
trouble falling asleep, get up, keep the lights low, and do something
you find relaxing. Just not in bed. You can stay in the bedroom if you
have a comfy chair; otherwise, go into another room. Read a book
or article, but not on a screen (remember, we're staying away from
screens a half hour before bed, as they can keep us awake). Maybe
write some lines in your journal. Or, if you have a dog or a cat, give
them some gentle pets.

By changing your environment, you're sending yourself a message
that your bed is for sleeping, not for being awake. In other words, getting

into bed should trigger a sleep response, not a work response. When we use our laptop in bed, then we aren't triggered to sleep; we're triggered to do some sort of work. After ten to twenty minutes, return to your bed and see whether you can go to sleep. If you can't, then try the military method or the deep relaxation method again. Do this whenever you haven't fallen asleep after twenty minutes.

3. *Consider a nap*: If you start to get low energy toward midday, consider taking a nap. If possible, find a cozy place to lie down, snuggle into a soft blanket, and allow yourself to fall asleep gently. A short nap, no longer than an hour, earlier in the day can reduce your fatigue and boost your energy. Caution: The later in the day you take a nap, the more difficulty you might have falling asleep at your regular bedtime. Also, too long a nap one day might throw off your sleep schedule the next night.

Living a Life of Happiness and Meaning

When we suffer a great loss, our happiness decreases, but we may discover even greater meaning in our lives. Grief can strengthen our character. It can allow us to peer deep into our being, as well as the lives of others. As a result, we can gain greater understanding of ourselves and other people. By experiencing hardships along with joy, we develop strength and depth of character and discernment. By focusing on finding meaning and happiness in our lives and in the future, we gain balance and stability. Then we're better able to persevere. For this reason, we've included these additional exercises. Of course, you don't have to try them all, but we hope you'll try some of them. And if you don't feel like doing them now, since you are reading this, consider coming back later to see whether you might like to try one under different circumstances.

Please check out Appendix III ("Character Strengths") before you do the next two exercises.

1. *Strengthen your character*: Although we all have character strengths, they can become overshadowed by our grief symptoms. Choose a character strength from Appendix III that you might like to accentuate. For example, if your top character strength is love but you haven't been in contact with people you were close to for a while, call one of them and make a plan to spend time with them. Or if you love nature and one of your top character strengths is appreciation of beauty

and excellence, think about taking a trip to a park or another natural setting. When you're there, take special note of the beauty around you. Take a few pictures to remind you of the experience later. The goal is to use your character strength in a way you haven't done in a while to fortify it.

2. *Highlight your character strength*: Plan on featuring one of your character strengths and then follow through with your plan. For instance, if love of learning is one of your top character strengths, plan a visit to a library, a lecture, or a museum soon. Then do it. Or, if gratitude is one of your character strengths (it's also a core value), then consider expressing your gratitude by "paying it forward" and doing something kind for someone else. For instance, take a sick friend's dog for a walk, or bring them some tasty soup. Or both! You'll be displaying your core value *and* your character strength—but only *you* need to know.

When we're in mourning, we can feel like a shadow of our former selves. Those character strengths that we used to call on to get us through life can be eclipsed by depression, anxiety, and fear. Fortunately, when this happens, we can decrease our depression and anxiety by doing things to boost our character strengths. Including other people in our plans can restore important social relationships and increase our self-confidence and esteem. These are important steps for us to take toward living a healthy, happier, more meaningful life.

3. *Connect for a moment*: The next time you have a conversation with someone, give that person your undivided attention. It doesn't matter how long the conversation is. As you look the person in the eye, listen to what they are saying. Don't interrupt—unless you're short on time, and then be polite when you tell them you have to leave. It might be best to start small, like with a loved one before they go to or return from school or work or a visit. Or you can start with the clerk at the checkout counter. After your encounter, do you feel more connected to that person or that you learned something about them you didn't know before? Do you think they noticed you were really listening to them, and how do you think that made them feel?

4. *Spread the warmth*: Create three "warm" moments with someone you know—at home, work, shopping, or somewhere else. These warm moments can be simple, like hugging a friend, giving a sincere compliment to a coworker for doing a good job, telling someone you love them if you haven't done that in a while, or looking the person

behind the deli counter in the eye and thanking them with a warm smile for their service (but only if you mean it). What may seem insignificant or unimportant can give both the recipient and the giver a happiness boost. Making such connections can increase our *mana* (life force) and help us feel more alive.

Grief can make it hard to focus on anything other than our loss. We may find that we aren't paying attention to conversations, people, reading material or whatever we may be viewing. And it's worse when someone points this inattentiveness out to us. But by taking the time to actively listen to others, we'll help train ourselves to pay better attention to the world around us and thus be more focused.

Active Listening

To practice being an active listener:

1. *Focus on what's being said.* Really listen to what the speaker is saying. Use eye contact and pay attention to body language and emotion.

2. *Repeat back.* Repeat to the speaker, in your own words, what you just heard. If the speaker says you got it wrong, ask the speaker to try again using different words; repeat this step until you understand what they are saying.

3. *Include emotions.* If the speaker is conveying strong emotion, then acknowledge it: "I understand you are angry/confused/hurt about _____." By doing so, the speaker knows you realize how they feel about what they are saying to you. Be empathetic and nonjudgmental—never condescending.

4. *Your turn.* Through active listening, you'll have a deeper understanding of where the other person is coming from and very likely a better view of the situation or problem. This knowledge may open the door to better communication and, in turn, to creating a better relationship between you two. When it's your turn to speak, stay open-minded and work toward possible solutions.

---

5. *Share your talent*: Choose something you like to do (for instance, baking or gardening), and then consider how you can share your talent and make it more meaningful. Whatever you do can be simple or involved. If you like to bake, make a big batch of something, or try baking something more complicated and share whatever you've made with family and friends. If you love to garden, construct an herb garden either in pots or in your yard and share your bounty with neighbors

and coworkers. Being productive in this way can make you happier (and certainly bring smiles to those receiving gifts).

6. *Giving back*: Volunteering is a wonderful way to add greater meaning to our lives. You may already be doing this, but if you aren't, consider what you might like to do and who would benefit from the gift of your personal, precious time. Consider working a few hours a week at a food bank. Maybe training others in a skill that you have would be appealing, or perhaps volunteering at a nearby animal shelter or being a school crossing guard. Whatever you may choose to do, it's an excellent way to start toward your brighter future. Sharing your talent and gifts with others gives greater meaning to your daily life.

Mourning and loss can cause us to overlook meaningful things. When we create new, significant experiences, we open ourselves up to what we thought we might have lost or, worse, never had: a meaningful life.

7. *Do something for you*: Think about something you enjoy doing and allow yourself to do it—guilt free! This can be something you do with others or on your own. Maybe you'd like to read a book all afternoon, or binge watch a favorite TV show, or have dinner with friends, or participate in a sport you haven't felt like playing since your loss. Maybe now it's time to start enjoying your life once again—or more fully.

Our self-esteem can take a dive after a devastating loss or traumatic event. We can lose our ability to experience joy and happiness. And when we do find ourselves having fun, we can feel guilty. But bringing joy back into our lives is one of the most important things we can do to live a more meaningful life. So let's start small and work our way to larger pursuits, especially those that can benefit others.

8. *Do something with others*: This exercise is similar to the one above, but it isn't a solo mission; it *must* include others. Plan something you'd enjoy doing with at least one other person, but two or more could be even better. What you choose to do can be passive (like going to a movie or a concert or having a meal), or it can be active (like hiking or flower arranging or playing a sport or game). Enjoy being a selective present hedonist!

As mentioned previously, when we mourn, we can lose track of important people in our lives. But when we reconnect with them, we can rediscover the joyous part within us that we have put aside since our loss. People seem to enjoy doing things with other people more than when they do the activity on their own. By consciously appreciating and enjoying these experiences, we are creating past positive memories to add to our treasure trove, ones that we can continue to draw on throughout our lives.

9. *Send a thank-you card*: Did you know that people who are grateful experience less depression and less stress and are happier than those who aren't so grateful? Let's practice gratitude by thinking of someone in our life for whom we are grateful. This individual could be a friend, a relative, a coworker or maybe a teacher or a person you know through your religious practice, someone who has been kind to you or others. It could even be a group of people who have helped you or someone you love, like a medical staff or the staff at an animal shelter. Your gratitude can be in general or for a specific act of kindness. Try to fill a thank-you card or a piece of paper with your written gratitude. Then pop it in the mail or hand deliver it. Maybe leave it on the person's desk or somewhere they'll be sure to see it. But if for some reason it doesn't feel right to send the card or note, that's okay. Put it aside. Just doing this exercise can improve your feelings of thankfulness.

Grateful people have more satisfying relationships with friends and family. They have higher self-esteem, along with better coping skills, and feel in control of their lives. Researcher Sonja Lyubormirsky conducted a study in which participants were asked to write a letter of gratitude to someone they wished to thank; in some instances, they hand delivered the letter to that person. (Just like our exercise above!) Immediate increases in happiness and decreases in depression were reported by the participants. (If you choose to thank a family member, friend, or coworker, you could be creating a more powerful bond between the two of you.)

10. *The importance of hydration*: We've discussed this topic at the beginning of the book, but it's worth another mention here at the end—with a slight twist. It's easy to forget about ourselves in important ways when we're grieving. We may not be eating properly or keeping hydrated. So in this exercise let's focus on the latter: hydration. According to Dr. Len Kravitz, professor of exercise science at the University of New Mexico, water is perhaps *the* most important nutrient. If we aren't drinking enough water, then increasing our intake can lower depression and anxiety. It can also improve our cognitive function. Our request to you: carry a bottle of water around with you wherever you go to help ensure that you're drinking the recommended amount (see the next paragraph). We can also do our diet a favor by replacing sugary beverages with a couple of glasses of water. By adding

things like citrus, berries, cucumber or electrolytes to our water, we can make it more delicious, reduce our calorie intake, hydrate our bodies, and improve our health.

Bear with us for a moment as we nerd out: That old eight 8-ounce cups a day recommendation for water consumption can be traced to a 1945 publication by the Food and Nutrition Board of the National Research Council. It's very outdated. One of the more recent studies on how much water or fluid we should ingest took place in 2004. This scientific study was conducted by the Institute of Medicine and published under the title "Dietary Reference Intake for Water." The study took into consideration the amount of water we lose each day through breathing, perspiring, bowel movements, and urine. The findings are that the *average man should drink thirteen cups* (that's eight ounces a cup) *of fluid* and the *average woman nine cups*. In liters, that's 3.0 liters for men and 2.2 for women.

More recently, this study seems to have opened the floodgates for other institutions and universities to conduct their own research. For instance, the Institute of Medicine of the National Academies recommends drinking *eleven cups* (2.7 liters) *for women* and *fifteen cups* (3.7 liters) *for men*. Now that we have some new parameters, let's try to consume somewhere *between nine and eleven cups of water for women* and *thirteen to fifteen cups for men*. So drink up and live healthier every day!

To Sum Up

- Thinking about the future can help us make wiser decisions, motivate us to achieve our goals, improve our psychological well-being, and make us kinder and more generous.
- Spending two hours a week in nature—either all at once or spaced out over several visits—can improve both our physical and our psychological well-being. Growing living plants and flowers or tending to a potted herb garden are ways to bring nature into our home and work environments.
- According to hundreds of studies conducted over several decades, music reduces stress and depression and can improve the way our immune systems work. Preliminary studies indicate that sound therapy—listening to Tibetan bowls—can also reduce stress, depression, pain, and blood pressure, while stimulating the immune system; however, more research is needed on this subject.

- When we are having a hard time coping, there are things we can do to help, such as being kind to ourselves by cutting down on screen time, taking mini-breaks throughout the day, and practicing random acts of kindness. Shifting our focus onto others in a good way is helpful in getting us out of a funk. We can express our love tangibly, notice the beauty around us, and be grateful for everything.
- When we are grieving, deep reflection is an important step to take to be our "better selves." It can help us leave behind our old baggage and better prepare us for whatever our "new" future holds for us.
- The four steps in ho'oponopono are remorse, forgiveness, gratitude, and love.
- In general, future-oriented people do very well in their lives; they are less aggressive and less depressed, have more energy, take care of their health, and have better impulse control and more self-esteem. They don't pay much attention to past experiences and can turn off the fracas of the present.
- It is possible for a future-oriented person to become *temporarily* stuck in a past negative or present fatalistic time perspective due to grief.
- It is also possible to be *too* future oriented. If we are one of these folks, we can be extreme multitaskers or, worse, workaholics.
- Being self-aware—consciously knowing our emotions, motives, and desires—is possibly the most important step toward generating a more positive present and a brighter future. When we are more self-aware, we realize that this new future may be very different from the future we had planned before our loss.
- Setting goals can be difficult when we are mourning. Things we had planned for the future may have changed or don't have the meaning they did before. But when we plan and accomplish smaller, short-term goals, we're better able to build on these skills until we are planning and accomplishing longer-term goals.
- For the most part, our experiences help us make informed decisions. But sometimes negative experiences can hold us back from doing something in the future. When we anticipate an event positively, we can boost our optimism. Optimistic people can persevere during difficult times and have good coping skills.
- Grief can disrupt our sleep cycle. Fortunately, different relaxation and/or sleep-encouraging techniques can help us attain more restful sleep.

- Our happiness decreases when we've suffered a great loss. However, grief may cause us to experience even greater meaning in our lives. Grief can strengthen our character and allow us to gain greater understanding of ourselves and other people. Hardships, along with joy, develop strength and depth of character as well as discernment. When we find meaning and happiness in our lives—and in the future—we gain stability and balance.
- When we are grateful, we enjoy a more satisfying relationship with those close to us. Grateful people feel like they are in control of their lives, have better coping skills, and possess higher self-esteem.
- Drinking the proper amount of water each day can lower anxiety and depression and improve our cognitive function.

References

Allen, S. (2019, May 1). How thinking about the future makes life more meaningful. *Greater Good Magazine.* https://greatergood.berkeley.edu/article/item/how_thinking_about_the_future_makes_life_more_meaningful.

Baloyi, L., & Makobe-Rabothata, M. (2014). The African conception of death: A cultural implication. In L.T.B. Jackson, D. Meiring, F.J.R. Van de Vijver, E.S. Idemoudia, & W.K. Gabrenya, Jr. (Eds.), *Toward sustainable development through nurturing diversity: Proceedings from the 21st International Congress of the International Association for Cross-Cultural Psychology.* https://scholarworks.gvsu.edu/cgi/viewcontent.cgi?article=1018&context=iaccp_papers#:~:text=In%20traditional%20African%20thought%20of,and%20how%20they%20have%20died.

Benson, D.E. (2018). Tlingit. *Encyclopedia.com.* https://www.encyclopedia.com/history/united-states-and-canada/north-american-indigenous-peoples/tlingit.

Central Council of the Tlingit and Haida Indian Tribes of Alaska. (n.d.). 40 Day Party/Koo.eex. https://www.ccthita.org/info/events/calendars/2023.MEMORIAL%20CALENDAR%20party%20format.pdf.

Charlot, J.P. (n.d.). Polynesian religions. *Encyclopedia of Death and Dying.* http://www.deathreference.com/Nu-Pu/Polynesian-Religions.html.

Cherry, K., & Klimenko, E. (2023, April 10). Can Tibetan singing bowls help reduce stress? *Very Well Mind.* https://www.verywellmind.com/tibetan-singing-bowls-for-healing-89828.

Coates, H. (2023, March 21). This is the military-approved trick that will help you fall asleep in minutes. *Vogue.* https://www.vogue.com/article/military-method-trick-for-sleeping.

Funeral Guide Staff. (2016, October 14). *Death around the world: Native American beliefs.* Funeral Guide. https://www.funeralguide.co.uk/blog/death-around-world-native-american-beliefs.

Funeral Guide Staff. (2016, December 9). Death around the world: Aboriginal funerals. *Funeral Guide.* https://www.funeralguide.co.uk/blog/death-around-the-world-australia.

Gould, W.R., & Monoahan, M. (2023). What is a sound bath? *Very Well Mind.* https://www.verywellmind.com/what-are-sound-baths-4783501.

Grant, A.M., & Berry, J.W. (2011). The necessity of others is the mother of invention:

Intrinsic and prosocial motivations, perspective taking, and creativity. *Academy of Management Journal, 54*(1), 73–96.

Grant, A.M., & Sonnentag, S. (2010). Doing good buffers against feeling bad: Prosocial impact compensates for negative task and self-evaluations. *Organizational Behavior and Human Decision Processes, 111*(1), 13–22.

Halverson-Ramos, F. (n.d.). Music therapy and mental health. *Soundwell Music Therapy.* https://soundwellmusictherapy.com/music-therapy-for-mental-health/.

Headey, B. (2007, July 3). Life goals matter to happiness: A revision of set-point theory. *Social Indicators Research, 86,* 213–31.

Institute of Medicine. (2004). Dietary reference intakes for water, potassium, sodium, chloride, and sulfate. https://nap.nationalacademies.org/read/10925/chapter/1.

Kane, H. K. (2014). The ʻaumakua—Hawaiian ancestral spirits. https://dlnr.hawaii.gov/sharks/files/2014/07/APaperbyHerbKane.pdf.

Korff, J. (2023). Sorry business: Mourning an Aboriginal death. *Creative Spirits.* https://www.creativespirits.info/aboriginalculture/people/mourning-an-aboriginal-death.

Kravitz, L. (n.d.). Water: Nature's most important nutrient. *University of New Mexico.* https://www.unm.edu/~lkravitz/Article%20folder/WaterUNM.html#.

Marcelino, U. (2021, October 20). Rare access captures dances and feasts of Amazonian chief's funeral ritual. *The Wider Image* (Reuters). https://www.reuters.com/investigates/special-report/brazil-indigenous-kuarup/.

McLaughlin, M. (2014). *Aperçus: The aphorisms of Mignon McLaughlin.* Portland, OR: BookBaby.

Northwest University Staff. (2020, January 18). What people who don't like music might tell us about social interaction. *Neuroscience News.* https://neurosciencenews.com/music-anhedonia-social-interaction-15518/#.

Novatny, A. (2013). Music as Medicine. *APA Monitor/Science Watch.* https://www.apa.org/monitor/2013/11/music.

Perry, C., & Gans, K. (2023, June 13). How much water should you drink a day, according to experts. *Forbes.* https://www.forbes.com/health/body/how-much-water-you-should-drink-per-day/.

Praghakar, J., & Hudson, J.A. (2014, November). The development of future thinking: Young children's ability to construct event sequences to achieve future goals. *Journal of Experimental Child Psychology, 127,* 95–109.

Propst, J. (2021, May 3). Culture and death: Asian Americans and Pacific Islanders. *Alive Hospice.* https://www.alivehospice.org/news-events/culture-and-death-asian-americans-and-pacific-islanders/#.

Quoidbach, J., Berry, E.V., Hansenne, M., & Mikolajczak, M. (2010, October). Positive emotion regulation and well-being: Comparing the impact of eight savoring and dampening strategies. *Personality and Individual Differences, 49*(5), 368–73.

Rosinger, A., & Herrick, K. (2016). Daily water intake among US men and women. *Centers for Disease Control & Prevention.* https://www.cdc.gov/nchs/products/databriefs/db242.htm#:~:text=Water%20is%20an%20essential%20nutrient,)%20for%20women%20(2).

Sealaska Heritage Institute. (n.d.). Ku.eex (Ceremonies). https://www.sealaskaheritage.org/sites/default/files/Unit%208_3.pdf.

Seligman, M.E. (2006). *Learned optimism: How to change your mind and your life.* New York, NY: Vintage.

Sheldon, K.M., & Lyubomirsky, S. (2006). How to increase and sustain positive emotion: The effects of expressing gratitude and visualizing best possible selves. *Journal of Positive Psychology, 1*(2), 73–82.

Spence, G.B., & Grant, A.M. (2007). Professional and peer life coaching and the enhancement of goal striving and well-being: An exploratory study. *Journal of Positive Psychology, 2*(3), 185–94.

Steger, M.F., Oishi, S., & Kashdan, T.B. (2009). Meaning in life across the life span: Levels and correlates of meaning in life from emerging adulthood to older adulthood. *Journal of Positive Psychology, 4*(1), 43–52.

Sword, R.K.M., & Zimbardo, P. (2021, November 21). Ho'oponopono: "To make things right." *Psychology Today.* https://www.psychologytoday.com/us/blog/the-time-cure/202111/ho-oponopono-make-things-right.

Sword, R.M., Sword, R.K.M., Brunskill, S.R., & Zimbardo, P.G. (2014). Time perspective therapy: A new time-based metaphor therapy for PTSD. *Journal of Loss and Trauma: International Perspectives on Stress & Coping, 19*(3), 197–201.

Tlingit & Haida Tribes of Alaska. (n.d.). Tlingit death ceremonies. *Central Council Tlingit & Haida Tribes of Alaska.* http://www.ccthita.org/about/overview/index.html.

United Nations Staff. (n.d.). Indigenous peoples. *United Nations.* https://www.un.org/en/fight-racism/vulnerable-groups/indigenous-peoples#.

V.P.S. Staff. (2022). Aboriginal culture and history. *Victorian Public Sector Commission.* https://vpsc.vic.gov.au/workforce-programs/aboriginal-cultural-capability-toolkit/-aboriginal-culture-and-history/.

White, M.P., Alcock, I., Grellier, J., Wheeler, B.W., Hartig, T., Warber, S.L., Bone, A., Depledge, M.H., & Fleming, L.E. (2019). Spending at least 120 minutes a week in nature is associated with good health and wellbeing. Scientific Reports/Springer. https://www.nature.com/articles/s41598-019-44097-3.

Willis, C.B., & Samuelson, M.C. (2020, October 30). Turn to nature with your grief. *Spirituality and Health.* https://www.spiritualityhealth.com/articles/2020/10/30/turn-to-nature-with-your-grief.

Wong, C., & Gans, S. (2023, May 4). What to know about music therapy. *Very Well Mind.* https://www.verywellmind.com/benefits-of-music-therapy-89829.

Zimbardo, P., & Boyd, J. *The time paradox: The new psychology of time that will change your life.* London, UK: Rider, 2008.

Zimbardo, P., & Sword, R.K.M. (2017). *Living and loving better: Healing from the past, embracing the present, creating an ideal future with time perspective therapy.* Jefferson, NC: McFarland.

Zimbardo, P., Sword, R.M., & Sword, R.K.M. (2012). *The time cure.* San Francisco, CA: Wiley.

From left: Phil Zimbardo, Rose Sword and Rick Sword at the University of Coimbra, Portugal, August 2012.

"Gone From My Sight"
—Henry Van Dyke

I am standing upon the seashore. A ship, at my side,
spreads her white sails to the moving breeze and starts for the blue ocean.
She is an object of beauty and strength.
I stand and watch her until, at length, she hangs like a speck
of white cloud just where the sea and sky come to mingle with each other.
Then, someone at my side says, "There, she is gone."
Gone where?
Gone from my sight. That is all.
She is just as large in mast, hull and spar as she was when she left my side.
And, she is just as able to bear her load of living freight to her destined port.
Her diminished size is in me—not in her.
And, just at the moment when someone says, "There, she is gone,"
there are other eyes watching her coming, and other voices
ready to take up the glad shout, "Here she comes!"
And that is dying…

Van Dyke, H. Gone from my sight. In B. Karnes (Ed.), *Gone from my sight: The dying experience*. Vancouver, WA: Barbara Karnes Publishing, 1986.

Epilogue

When we finished writing the "To Sum Up" section at the conclusion of Chapter Four, we knew we were at the end of this book. We'd presented what we had set out to share and hoped that offering a glimpse into our experiences—at work, in the clinic, and in our personal lives—would somehow be helpful. And yet we felt incomplete; we weren't ready to say "goodbye" to you just yet, especially in such an abrupt way. Not after what we'd just been through together.

Then, as we were working on final details before sending the book to our publisher, our personal editor, Andie Coutoumanos, and one of our "sparkers" pointed out that we had omitted newer, more modern burial practices. Nor had we included more updated methods for remembering the deceased, especially in situations where travel can be difficult. Further, if *they* wanted to know about such things, surely there would be other readers who would be equally interested. Happy to have a reason to continue our journey, even if only for a short jaunt, we dug into researching "modern" funerals and burial practices. After weeding out the more eccentric (and costly!) methods—cryonics, mummification, plastination, resomation, space burial and freeze drying—we focused on what we consider a good-for-us-and-the-planet theme.

Modern Burials: A Gift, a Celebration, and a Remembrance

In an article for *AARP*, journalist Leanne Pott shared that nowadays more people are opting to skip religious services and the burial of an embalmed body in a casket and are looking for more budget-friendly, easier-on-the-earth burials. This trend also includes more personal rituals, breaking rigid twentieth-century customs. In addition, Stephanie Pappas of *Live Science* reported on another method we had first heard about from an ocean science–minded friend. Along with these methods, we provide a few ways to honor a lost loved one.

CREMATION

In recent years, cremation has surpassed traditional burial. By 2030, it's estimated that 70 percent of burials will be by cremation, with that number increasing to nearly 80 percent by 2040. However, cremation has recently been getting some competition.

GREEN OR NATURAL BURIAL

This "new" type of burial is actually a return to the "old ways." The deceased is wrapped in a shroud (or placed in a biodegradable casket) and buried directly in the ground. Then nature takes over. The cost is about half that of a traditional burial—sometimes much less—and it is also better for the environment. Sometimes trees are planted above the body, and in some places, these burial grounds double as nature preserves.

ETERNAL REEFS

For those dialed into the sad conditions of some of our planet's coral reefs, this burial method may be appealing. The cost can be less than half as much as the average traditional burial. Eternal Reefs (*eternalreefs.com*) provides a "cremation urn" (the ashes are mixed with cement), burial at sea, and GPS coordinates. The cremation urn is placed on the seabed and quickly becomes a living reef that provides a much-needed habitat for sea life to flourish.

AT-HOME FUNERALS

More people are caring for their deceased loved one on their own, with the family washing and dressing the body, hosting an at-home viewing, and handling the burial themselves. This very personal type of burial is estimated to cost as little as $200 if the loved one is buried in the yard or on one's own property. If professional assistance is needed (for example, the body may need to be stored in ice packs), then funeral homes or other specialists can be invited to provide such help.

• • •

GIFTING CHARITY

You've no doubt heard of or participated in the modern custom of a family requesting that, instead of flowers, a donation be made to a favorite charity or cause on behalf of the deceased. This is a wonderful way to honor the wishes of the family and the departed, as well as help an organization in need.

CELEBRATION OF LIFE

These events are generally casual and less structured than a funeral, and the atmosphere may be more like a festive gathering. A celebration of life can happen months—or maybe even longer—after the death of the loved one, giving the organizers time to plan and attendees time to make travel arrangements if necessary. During the event, memories can be shared, trees or flowers may be planted, a playlist of the deceased's favorite tunes might be played, and perhaps lanterns or balloons could be released. In coastal areas, if the deceased loved the ocean or was a surfer, a paddle-out ceremony can be held in which people with flowers or lei paddle out on their surfboards or body boards. They form a circle and remember their loved one while releasing their lei or flowers. The ashes of the deceased might also be released into the water at that time.

REMEMBRANCE

On a set day at a set time, no matter where the mourners are in the world (remember to take time zones into consideration), a few minutes—for instance, fifteen—are put aside for quiet contemplation and acknowledgment of the passing of a loved one. When the individual or people in charge of the remembrance event notify others—whether through written communication (email, postal service, *Facebook*, and such) or over the phone—details such as the lighting of a candle, a meditation focused on appreciation of the deceased, a cherished song played or sung by the participants, the recitation of a specific prayer, or raising a glass of the deceased's favorite beverage should be shared so that all can participate at the same time. *Zoom* or *Skype* can be employed for a more intimate-gathering feel. This is a heartwarming and effective way for all to bond over the loss of a loved one, especially if, due to distance, far-flung family and friends are unable to attend a memorial service in person.

Epilogue

. . .

After the above (especially "Remembrance"), we feel better able to say "so long." We wish you a bright future, rich in both experience and love, as well as all the good things life has to offer. We leave you with a short inspirational poem:

"Butterfly Wings"
—Sabina Laura

We all need
some measure of comfort,
the safety of a cocoon,

But I remind myself
that change is good,
that I cannot spend
my whole life
being a caterpillar,

that courage
wears butterfly wings
and the sky has never looked
more inviting.

Source:

Laura, S. (2021, January). Butterfly wings. *Family Friend Poems*. https://www.family friendpoems.com/poem/butterfly-wings

References

Pappas, S. (2011). After death: 8 burial alternatives. *Live Science*. https://www.livescience.com/15980-death-8-burial-alternatives.html.

Pott, L. (2017, November 20). 6 funeral trends that are changing death rituals. *AARP*. https://www.aarp.org/home-family/friends-family/info-2017/funeral-ceremony-trends-fd.html.

Staff Writer. (n.d.). A celebration of life service—what you need to know. *Trust & Will*. https://trustandwill.com/learn/celebration-of-life.

Glossary

Balanced time perspective—Having free emotional and mental mobility between thoughts of the past, present, and future; the optimum psychological state. See *Time perspective(s)*.

Brighter future—A future time perspective free of emotional and mental suffering; the goal of time perspective therapy. It is the hope that the future will be better than the past.

Cognitive behavioral therapy—A systematic, goal-oriented psychotherapeutic approach merging two talk therapies: cognitive therapy (aimed at changing nonconstructive emotional responses and dysfunctional thinking) and behavioral therapy (reinforcing wanted behaviors and eliminating undesired behaviors).

Expanded present—This is the "absolute present," a concept central to Buddhism and meditation. Through daily meditation, one can experience being in the present moment, unfiltered through the lenses of the past or the future. In this perspective, the past, the present, the future, the physical, the mental, and the spiritual elements in life are not separate but closely interconnected within the practitioner.

Future—See *Time perspective(s)*.

Past negative—See *Time perspective(s)*.

Past positive—See *Time perspective(s)*.

Present fatalism—See *Time perspective(s)*.

Present hedonism—See *Time perspective(s)*.

Temporary present fatalism—When one is grieving, it's possible to have a *temporary present fatalistic* mindset due to current circumstances. For instance, ZTPI scores prior to the loss of a loved one may have been "normal" (i.e., high in past positive and future time perspectives). But due to the loss, a new ZTPI score may indicate high present fatalism. In time, one's natural, positive time perspective will most likely return, and the negative time perspective will recede.

Time perspective(s)—The psychological term for the process by which each of us sorts our personal experiences into temporal categories. Each of the three primary subjective time zones—past, present, and future—is divided into two parts, yielding six main time perspectives:

- *Past positive*—A positive focus on the memories of the good old days, family, and tradition.
- *Past negative*—A negative focus that recalls past abuse, failures, and regrets over missed opportunities.
- *Present hedonism*—A focus on pleasure, risk taking, and sensation seeking. Also of note:
  - *Selected present hedonism*—A focus on a moderate amount of pleasure and sensation seeking, frequently as a reward for accomplishments.
- *Present fatalism*—A focus on not taking control of situations that is driven by a belief that life is fated to play out in a certain way, no matter what one does.
- *Future*—A focus on working toward goals, meeting deadlines, and achieving objectives. In the development of time perspective therapy, the future time perspective is split into:
  - *Future positive/brighter future*—A focus on an optimistic future.
  - *Future negative/future fatalistic*—A focus on a defeatist future.
- *Transcendental future*—A focus that places spiritual life after the death of the body above all else (religious); a focus that places the long-term future of many generations, or the life of the planet, above all else (secular).

Time perspective therapy (TPT)—The implementation of Zimbardo's Temporal Theory in clinical practice, using a context of time perspectives; an evolution of cognitive behavioral therapy. Developed by Richard and Rosemary Sword in 2008–2009, it has been used successfully to treat PTSD, depression, anxiety and stress, in addition to being used in individual, couples, family and grief counseling.

Transcendental future—See *Time perspective(s)*.

Zimbardo's Temporal Theory—The theory that one's time perspective(s) affect one's view of one's life and choices. Temporal theory, as posited by Philip Zimbardo, stresses the importance of one's individual time perspective and its impact on one's sense of mental distress or well-being. Being stuck in one or two negative time perspectives of the six possible time perspectives seems to be a critical factor in emotional distress; a balanced time perspective is the cornerstone of emotional well-being.

ZTPI (Zimbardo Time Perspective Inventory)—The 56-item scale (or 15-item short-form scale) used for measuring one's time perspective in five factors: past negative, past positive, present fatalistic, present hedonistic, future. The ZTPI is the main tool used in TPT to determine whether an individual's time perspectives are balanced or unbalanced.

APPENDIX I

ZTPI Questionnaire

(Long Form)

1—Very Untrue
2—Untrue
3—Neutral
4—True
5—Very True

1. I believe that getting together with one's friends to party is one of life's important pleasures... _____

2. Familiar childhood sights, sounds, and smells often bring back a flood of wonderful memories... _____

3. Fate determines much in my life... _____

4. I often think of what I should have done differently in my life.. _____

5. My decisions are mostly influenced by people and things around me .... _____

6. I believe that a person's day should be planned ahead each morning.. _____

7. It gives me pleasure to think of my past .... _____

8. I do things impulsively .... _____

9. If things don't get done on time, I don't worry about it.............. _____

10. When I want to achieve something, I set goals and consider specific means for reaching those goals....................................... _____

11. On balance, there is much more good to recall than bad in my past .... _____

12. When listening to my favorite music, I often lose all track of time .... _____

13. Meeting tomorrow's deadlines and doing other necessary work come before tonight's play .... ____

14. Since whatever will be will be, it doesn't really matter what I do .... ____

15. I enjoy stories about how things used to be in the "good old days" .... ____

16. Painful past experiences keep being replayed in my mind .... ____

17. I try to live my life as fully as possible, one day at a time .... ____

18. It upsets me to be late for appointments .... ____

19. Ideally, I would live each day as if it were my last .... ____

20. Happy memories of good times spring readily to mind .... ____

21. I meet my obligations to friends and authorities on time .... ____

22. I've taken my share of abuse and rejection in the past .... ____

23. I make decisions on the spur of the moment .... ____

24. I take each day as it is rather than try to plan it out .... ____

25. The past has too many unpleasant memories that I prefer not to think about .... ____

26. It is important to put excitement in my life .... ____

27. I've made mistakes in the past that I wish I could undo .... ____

28. I feel it's more important to enjoy what you are doing than to get work done on time .... ____

29. I get nostalgic about my childhood .... ____

30. Before making a decision, I weigh the costs against the benefits .... ____

31. Taking risks keeps my life from becoming boring .... ____

32. It is more important for me to enjoy life's journey than to focus only on the destination .... ____

33. Things rarely work out as I expected .... ____

34. It's hard for me to forget unpleasant images of my youth .... ____

35. It takes joy out of the process and flow of my activities if I have to think about goals, outcomes, and products .... ____

36. Even when I am enjoying the present, I am drawn back to comparisons with similar past experiences .... ____

37. You can't really plan for the future because things change so much... _____

38. My life path is controlled by forces I cannot influence............... _____

39. It doesn't make sense to worry about the future, since there is nothing that I can do about it anyway........................... _____

40. I complete projects on time by making steady progress............. _____

41. I find myself tuning out when family members talk about the way things used to be .... _____

42. I take risks to put excitement in my life .... _____

43. I make lists of things to do .... _____

44. I often follow my heart more than my head............................... _____

45. I am able to resist temptations when I know that there is work to be done .... _____

46. I find myself getting swept up in the excitement of the moment.. _____

47. Life today is too complicated; I would prefer the simpler life of the past .... _____

48. I prefer friends who are spontaneous rather than predictable.. _____

49. I like family traditions and rituals that are regularly repeated .... _____

50. I think about the bad things that have happened to me in the past .... _____

51. I keep working at difficult, uninteresting tasks if they will help me get ahead .... _____

52. Spending what I earn on pleasure today is better than saving for tomorrow's security .... _____

53. Often luck pays off better than hard work .... _____

54. I think about the good things that I have missed out on in my life.. _____

55. I like my close relationships to be passionate .... _____

56. There will always be time to catch up on my work...................... _____

ZTPI Scoring Key

Before scoring the ZTPI, you have to reverse the answers for questions 9, 24, 25, 41, and 56:

1 becomes a 5
2 becomes a 4
3 remains a 3
4 becomes a 2
5 becomes a 1

After reversing these answers, add the scores for the questions that make up each time perspective. Next, divide the total score for each section by the number of questions that make up each time perspective. This results in an average score for each of the five time perspectives.

The Past Negative Time Perspective

Add the scores for questions 4, 5, 16, 22, 27, 33, 34, 36, 50, and 54. Then divide this number by 10.

QUESTIONS

4. I often think of what I should have done differently in my life..... _____

5. My decisions are mostly influenced by people and things around me .... _____

16. Painful past experiences keep being replayed in my mind .... _____

22. I've taken my share of abuse and rejection in the past .... _____

27. I've made mistakes in the past that I wish I could undo .... _____

33. Things rarely work out as I expected .... _____

34. It's hard for me to forget unpleasant images of my youth .... _____

36. Even when I am enjoying the present, I am drawn back to comparisons with similar past experiences .... _____

50. I think about the bad things that have happened to me in the past... _____

54. I think about the good things that I have missed out on in my life.. _____

Score: _____

The Past Positive Time Perspective

Add the scores for questions 2, 7, 11, 15, 20, 25 (reversed*), 29, 41 (reversed*), and 49. (*1 = 5; 2 = 4; 3 = 3; 4 = 2; 5 = 1) Then divide this number by 9.

QUESTIONS

2. Familiar childhood sights, sounds, and smells often bring back a flood of wonderful memories.. _____

7. It gives me pleasure to think of my past .... _____

11. On balance, there is much more good to recall than bad in my past... _____

15. I enjoy stories about how things used to be in the "good old days"... _____

20. Happy memories of good times spring readily to mind............ _____

25. The past has too many unpleasant memories that I prefer not to think about.. _____

29. I get nostalgic about my childhood .... _____

41. I find myself tuning out when family members talk about the way things used to be... _____

49. I like family traditions and rituals that are regularly repeated..... _____

Score: _____

The Present Fatalistic Time Perspective

Add the scores for questions 3, 14, 35, 37, 38, 39, 47, 52, and 53. Then divide this number by 9.

QUESTIONS

3. Fate determines much in my life .... _____

14. Since whatever will be will be, it doesn't really matter what I do .... _____

35. It takes joy out of the process and flow of my activities if I have to think about goals, outcomes, and products .... _____

37. You can't really plan for the future because things change so much .... _____

38. My life path is controlled by forces I cannot influence.............. _____

39. It doesn't make sense to worry about the future, since there is nothing that I can do about it anyway .... _____

47. Life today is too complicated; I would prefer the simpler life of the past .... _____

52. Spending what I earn on pleasure today is better than saving for tomorrow's security... _____

53. Often luck pays off better than hard work .... _____

   Score: _____

The Present Hedonistic Time Perspective

Add the scores for questions 1, 8, 12, 17, 19, 23, 26, 28, 31, 32, 42, 44, 46, 48, and 55. Then divide this number by 15.

QUESTIONS

 1. I believe that getting together with one's friends to party is one of life's important pleasures... _____

 8. I do things impulsively .... _____

12. When listening to my favorite music, I often lose all track of time .... _____

17. I try to live my life as fully as possible, one day at a time .... _____

19. Ideally, I would live each day as if it were my last .... _____

23. I make decisions on the spur of the moment .... _____

26. It is important to put excitement in my life .... _____

28. I feel it's more important to enjoy what you are doing than to get work done on time .... _____

31. Taking risks keeps my life from becoming boring...................... _____

32. It is more important for me to enjoy life's journey than to focus only on the destination .... _____

42. I take risks to put excitement in my life .... _____

44. I often follow my heart more than my head................................. _____

46. I find myself getting swept up in the excitement of the moment .... _____

48. I prefer friends who are spontaneous rather than predictable... _____
55. I like my close relationships to be passionate .... _____

   Score: _____

The Future Time Perspective

Add the scores for questions 6, 9 (reversed*), 10, 13, 18, 21, 24 (reversed*), 30, 40, 43, 45, 51, and 56 (reversed*). (*1 = 5; 2 = 4; 3 = 3; 4 = 2, 5 = 1) Then divide this number by 13.

QUESTIONS

6. I believe that a person's day should be planned ahead each morning.. _____

9. If things don't get done on time, I don't worry about it.............. _____

10. When I want to achieve something, I set goals and consider specific means for reaching those goals.. _____

13. Meeting tomorrow's deadlines and doing other necessary work come before tonight's play.................................... _____

18. It upsets me to be late for appointments .... _____

21. I meet my obligations to friends and authorities on time........... _____

24. I take each day as it is rather than try to plan it out.................... _____

30. Before making a decision, I weigh the costs against the benefits.... _____

40. I complete projects on time by making steady progress............. _____

43. I make lists of things to do .... _____

45. I am able to resist temptations when I know that there is work to be done .... _____

51. I keep working at difficult, uninteresting tasks if they will help me get ahead.. _____

56. There will always be time to catch up on my work...................... _____

Score: _____

My ZTPI Scores

Past negative: _____
Past positive: _____
Present fatalism: _____
Present hedonism: _____
Future: _____

ZTPI Graph

Plot the scores on the ideal time perspective graph provided below. Draw a line from past negative to past positive, from past positive to present fatalism, and so on. Compare your score with the ideal time perspective shown here.

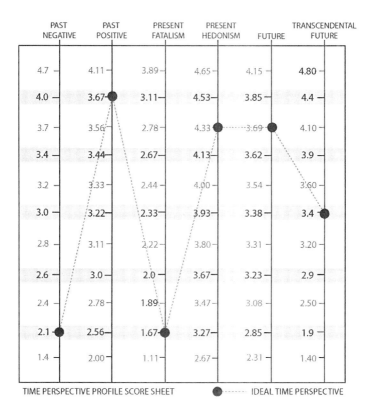

TIME PERSPECTIVE PROFILE SCORE SHEET   ●······· IDEAL TIME PERSPECTIVE

Plot your ZTPI time perspective scores on this graph and compare them to the ideal.

Core Values

A quick online search of "core values" will lead you to a wealth of sites and articles about this subject, which are sometimes called "personal values." You'll also find that many of the sites are work related because in the 1980–1990s, the idea of personal core values was slowly adapted for corporations as well as the workplace. (As an aside, values—also known as "ethics"—have been around for thousands of years, most likely starting with the Chinese philosopher Confucius around 500 BCE. However, Confucius was upholding values of much earlier philosophers from the Xia dynasty from over 4,000 years ago!)

Our search uncovered lists that had over 500 core values, which is overwhelming. For our purposes here, we'll focus on thirty personal core values using some examples of a few professionals, including author and psychologist Steven Stosny and Dr. Chris Drew of *Helpfulprofessor.com*.

Love, a core value that was difficult to find on the numerous lists we reviewed, kicks off *our* list. It is followed by seven more core values that support love as a core value in relationships. The rest are presented in alphabetical order. Most of these core values are personal, but some can be expanded to include groups of people or organizations.

• • •

Core values are developed from our cultural and social environment. In other words, our current values are passed down from generation to generation through our families, cultures, and societies. Another important source of core values for many people is religion. Numerous religions encourage people to adopt core values such as charity, goodwill, and justice.

Examples of Core Values

1. *Love*: To us, this is the most important core value. We may tend to put the love we have for people and things all together in one big

lump. But thousands of years ago, the philosopher Aristotle taught that there were different types of friendships. In time, this train of thought evolved into different types of love. (*Note:* Empathy is also a separate core value.)

- Empathy—placing yourself in another person's position or situation and understanding or feeling what the other person is experiencing.
- Friendship—mutual affection shared between people. It's a stronger bond than being an "acquaintance" (such as a classmate, colleague, coworker, or neighbor).
- Romantic love—a powerful attraction and deep emotional feelings toward another person (which may include idealization) that can result in a bonded relationship.
- Unconditional love—considered the highest form of love, this emotion (also known as *agape*) is a transcendent love that exists regardless of situation or conditions. Religiously, it is often described as the love God has for humanity and humanity for God.

2. *Family*: Family values are the moral and ethical principles of typical family life, including making sacrifices for loved ones, putting your loved ones first, sharing burdens as well as commodities, and keeping your loved ones at the center of your thoughts and actions.

3. *Equality*: The belief that rights, preferences, opportunities, and responsibilities are (or should be) more or less equal.

4. *Fairness*: Maintaining a mutually acceptable division of labor and responsibility for the growth and well-being of the couple/family and others.

5. *Goodwill*: Wanting the best for everyone.

6. *Cooperation*: Working together for the best interests of the couple/family and others.

7. *Flexibility*: Seeing the other person's side and working toward compromise; when rigidity is replaced with flexibility, it also allows for greater adaptation when unexpected situations arise.

8. *Appreciation*: A feeling of admiration, approval, or gratitude; it is acceptance of differences and giving someone (or something) their proper value.

• • •

9. *Altruism*: The practice of selfless concern for the welfare of other human beings or animals. It is a traditional virtue in many cultures and a core aspect of various religious and secular worldviews.

10. *Compassion*: Being sensitive to the emotional aspects of the suffering and misfortunes of other people and animals. Ideally, these positive sentiments are transformed into social actions that help others.

11. *Compromise*: Seeking agreement with others that involves some sort of divergence from your original goal but can achieve greater outcomes for all involved.

12. *Empathy*: Placing yourself in someone else's position and understanding and feeling what they are experiencing from their point of view, not your own.

13. *Environmentalism*: The belief that the environment and natural world is extremely important for the survival of the planet and should be protected against negative human impacts.

14. *Forgiveness*: The intentional decision to release resentment and anger. Forgiveness is a central value in major religious and spiritual beliefs, as it emphasizes the importance of redemption.

15. *Generosity*: Being liberal in giving away one's time and resources, often to people in need. Generosity is considered a virtue in many world religions and philosophies, and it is often celebrated in cultural and religious ceremonies. It can also mean giving compliments and praise when deserved.

16. *Gratitude*: Feeling appreciation when someone is kind and sincerely expressing that thankfulness; not taking for granted your own well-being. It also applies to the ability to observe and appreciate the goodness all around us, even during challenging times (in a more religious context, "counting your blessings").

17. *Honesty*: A virtuous quality that encompasses other core values (some covered in this list and some we don't), such as fairness, integrity, loyalty, trustworthiness, straightforwardness, and sincerity. It also implies an absence of lying, cheating, theft, and so on.

18. *Humility*: Free from pride or arrogance; a modest view of your own importance.

19. *Integrity*: Having strong moral and ethical principles and values; acting with honesty and adhering to your own moral code regardless of what others do.

20. *Kindness*: Being friendly, generous, and considerate; freely giving assistance or having concern for others, without expecting praise or

reward in return; being gentle with criticism and always willing to welcome people (even strangers) with open arms.

21. *Loyalty*: Devotion, faithfulness, or attachment to a person, people, an ideal, duty, or cause.

22. *Open-Mindedness*: Receptivity to new ideas; willingness to hear new points of view and even change your own point of view if new arguments are highly convincing. (It's the opposite of stubbornness.)

23. *Optimism*: Hopefulness and confidence about the future or that outcomes in general will be favorable. Being optimistic allows one to persevere through hard times.

24. *Patience*: Accepting difficult circumstances or slower results without getting angry, disrespectful, or upset; this includes working with people—especially children—or tasks that may require additional unanticipated effort.

25. *Perseverance*: Continuing to work toward achieving a goal despite difficulties, failure, or opposition.

26. *Respect*: Accepting someone for who they are, even when they don't agree with you or are different from you; also a sense of admiration.

27. *Self-Discipline*: Controlling your feelings in order to overcome weaknesses; being able to pursue what you think is right despite the urge to quit.

28. *Social Justice*: The perspective that all people deserve equal economic, political, and social rights, privileges, and opportunities within a society.

29. *Thoughtfulness*: Consideration for the needs of others.

30. *Tolerance and Diversity*: Respect, acceptance, and appreciation for the rich diversity of our world's cultures, our forms of expression, and our many ways of being human.

References

Ahmed, A. (2021, February 23). A history of research into core values. *Values Institute*. https://values.institute/a-history-of-research-into-core-values/.

Drew, C. (2023, September 12). 35 personal values examples. *Helpful Professor*. https://helpfulprofessor.com/personal-values-examples/.

Harris, L. (2020, September 21). Six steps to identify and align your personal core values. *Forbes*. https://www.forbes.com/sites/forbescoachescouncil/2020/09/21/six-steps-to-identify-and-align-your-personal-core-values.

Lewis, C.S. (1960). *The four loves*. London, UK: Geoffrey Bles.

Stosny, S. (2013, January 14). Love and values. *Psychology Today*. https://www.psychologytoday.com/us/blog/anger-in-the-age-entitlement/201301/love-and-values.

Appendix III

Character Strengths

All of us have character strengths, and everyone can use them. Character strengths are ways through which we express our core or personal values. They help us strive toward the things we find most meaningful. Courtney Ackerman is the author of several books on positive psychology. In an online article titled "15 Character Strength Examples, Interventions & Worksheets," she put together a list of six main "virtues" (also known as core values). These six qualities have emerged across the world and throughout time. Further, she notes that within each of these values are numerous character strengths that relate to demonstrating that particular core value.

What follows is a list of six universal core values along with the character strengths they display:

- Wisdom and knowledge—sound judgment; ability to discern hidden truths; understanding of the world
  - Creativity—the use of the imagination or original ideas, especially in the production of an artistic work
  - Curiosity—a strong desire to learn or know something
  - Open-mindedness—willing to learn new ideas; unprejudiced
  - Love of learning—passion for learning; desire to learn for learning's sake
  - Perspective—a particular attitude toward or way of regarding something; a point of view
- Courage—the ability to do something that frightens one; strength in the face of pain or grief
  - Bravery—courageous behavior or character
  - Persistence—continuing in a course of action in spite of difficulty or opposition
  - Integrity—the quality of being honest and having strong moral principles; moral uprightness
  - Vitality—the state of being strong and active; energy

- Humanity—the human race; human beings collectively; humaneness; benevolence
  ◦ Love—an intense feeling of deep affection (See item 1 in Appendix II)
  ◦ Kindness—the quality of being friendly, generous, and considerate
  ◦ Social intelligence—the capacity to know oneself and others
- Justice—appropriate behavior or treatment; based on or behaving according to what is morally right and fair
  ◦ Citizenship—the position or status of being a citizen of a particular country; allegiance
  ◦ Fairness—impartial and just treatment or behavior without favoritism or discrimination
  ◦ Leadership—the action of leading a group of people or an organization; the state or position of being a leader
- Moderation/Temperance—the avoidance of excess or extremes, especially in one's behavior or political opinions; self-restraint
  ◦ Forgiveness and mercy—the action or process of forgiving or being forgiven (See item 14 in Appendix II)
  ◦ Humility/Modesty—self-effacement; unassuming or moderate in the estimation of one's abilities (See item 18 in Appendix II)
  ◦ Prudence—cautiousness; using judgment
  ◦ Self-regulation—regulating oneself without intervention from external bodies
- Transcendence—existence or experience beyond the normal or physical level
  ◦ Appreciation of beauty and excellence—feeling powerful transcendent emotions when noticing beauty in the world
  ◦ Gratitude—the quality of being thankful; readiness to show appreciation for and to return kindness (See item 16 in Appendix II)
  ◦ Hope/Optimism—a feeling of expectation and desire for a certain thing to happen; confidence about the future (See item 23 in Appendix II)
  ◦ Humor—the quality of being amusing or comic, especially as expressed in literature or speech; a mood or state of mind
  ◦ Spirituality—the quality of being concerned with the human spirit or soul, as opposed to material or physical things; the recognition of a feeling or sense or belief that there is

something greater than oneself, something more to being human than sensory experience, and that the greater whole of which humanity is part is cosmic or divine in nature

REFERENCES

Ackerman, C., & Nash, J. (2019, September 29). 15 character strength examples, interventions & worksheets. *Positive Psychology.* https://positivepsychology.com/character-strength-examples-interventions-worksheets/.

Oxford English Dictionary. Oxford, UK: Oxford University Press.

Spencer, M. (2012). *What is spirituality? A personal exploration.* London, UK: Royal College of Psychiatrists.

Resources

Grief

Alicia Forneret has created a corner of the internet for what she refers to as "a different approach to grief," which includes informative blog columns (https://alicaforneret.co/).

The Center for Prolonged Grief, geared toward COVID-19 situations, is designed more for professionals than the public; however, the website includes articles, webinars and podcasts for all (https://prolongedgrief.columbia.edu/).

Good Grief (a nonprofit website) includes tips, videos and support for those who have lost a loved one (https://good-grief.org/resources/).

Hospice Foundation of America is an excellent source of information on end-of-life situations, hospice care and grief (https://hospicefoundation.org/Hospice-Care).

March of Dimes is a nonprofit organization that works to improve the health of mothers and babies in the United States. Its website contains information about miscarriage as well as the loss of a baby, including a way to honor your loss (https://www.marchofdimes.org/find-support/topics/miscarriage-loss-and-grief).

Pathways Center for Grief and Loss provides a wealth of information in the form of links to the organization's online video library, COVID-19 guidance, grief and loss for adults, grief and loss for kids and teens, and much more (https://www.hospiceandcommunitycare.org/grief-and-loss/grief-links/).

The Shared Grief Project provides stories of people who have experienced a major loss at an early age and have gone on to live healthy, happy and successful lives (https://sharedgrief.org/).

Soaring Spirits helps widowed people cope with grief and connect with others who have lost a spouse (https://soaringspirits.org/).

What's Your Grief is an online community that provides hope, creative expression, support, and education to understand the complicated experience of life after loss (https://whatsyourgrief.com/).

Why Grief Matters was created for those who have lost a loved one during the COVID-19 pandemic; the website includes online resources on grief and loss (https://www.covidgriefresources.com/).

The World Health Organization is a specialized agency of the United Nations that is responsible for international public health. This article may be helpful if you've suffered a miscarriage or lost a baby (https://www.who.int/newsroom/spotlight/why-we-need-to-talk-about-losing-a-baby).

Other Helpful Sites

Happify provides science-based activities when you're feeling sad, anxious, or stressed. Happify is user friendly and utilizes techniques developed by leading scientists and experts in the fields of positive psychology, mindfulness, and cognitive behavioral therapy. It is good for those new to cognitive behavioral therapy and positive psychology. (Phil and Rose created four-week programs for people who have suffered a loss and are grieving, as well as for post-traumatic stress.) Check out the free apps at https://happify.com.

"How to Practice Active Listening": This article by Amanda O'Bryan and Christina Wilson includes a wealth of information, including links to videos and free courses on how to be an active listener (https://positivepsychology.com/active-listening-techniques/).

Suicide and Crisis Hotline (nationwide): In the United States, dial 988. The lifeline provides 24/7, free and confidential support for people in distress, including prevention and crisis resources for you or your loved ones (https://988lifeline.org).

Time Perspective Therapy–Related Sites

The River of Time: This soothing 20-minute time perspective therapy video—written by Rick and Rose Sword, narrated by Rose, and produced by Robert Masters of Twin Peaks Creative—can be viewed for free on YouTube (https://www.youtube.com/watch?v=r4ZX0XVAa2A&t=264s).

Rose and Phil's *Psychology Today* articles:
   1) Google "Rosemary Sword." Then, under the *Psychology Today* website, click on "Rosemary K.M. Sword and Philip Zimbardo Ph.D." Scroll down for our most recent articles. *OR*
   2) Enter this URL in your search bar: https://www.psychologytoday.com/us/contributors/rosemary-km-sword-and-philip-zimbardo-phd

The Time Paradox website: Take the 56-item Zimbardo Time Perspective Inventory (ZTPI) as well as the Transcendental-future Time Perspective Inventory (TTPI) at this website. Your time perspective results are automatically scored (https://www.thetimeparadox.com/surveys/).

Time Perspective Therapy—our official website (http://www.timeperspectivetherapy.org/).

Index

AARP (magazine) 149
abbreviated grief 12
abandonment 9, 33
Aboriginal 118–119
absent grief 12
abuse/abusines behavior 81- 82
Academy of Management Journal 144
acceptance 40, 41–42, 54, 59, 66, 127
Ackerman, Courtney 167, 169
active listening 138
addiction 27, 91, 96; addictive personality 31; drug/overdose 14, 15, 74, 91, 96; food 91, 96, 103; gambling 91, 103; internet 91, 103; news 116; self medication 14; sex 91, 103; shopping 91, 103; substance 14; video games 91, 103, 116
adult care centers 77
Afghanistan 95
Africa 20, 117, 118, 143
afterlife 84, 118, 119, 121
agape *see* love
agnostic 21–22
Ahmen, A. 166
alcoholism/abuse 14, 74, 91, 96, 103
Alcock, I. 146
Alive Hospice (*alivehospice.org*) 144
Allah 84
Allen, Summer 107, 143
alone 10, 33
altruism 165
Amazon 120
amends 122–123
American Cancer Society (ACS) 104
American Indigenous People 119–120, 122
American Psychiatric Association 48, 68
American Psychological Association 35, 67
America(s) 20, 38, 42, 66, 117, 119–125; Far North 120
ancestral selfhood 118
ancestral spirits 118, 120; *'aumakua* 121
anger and irritability 11, 40, 41, 47, 49, 54, 55, 56, 66, 74, 81, 82 97, 103, 115
Anglican *see* Christianity
anti-anxiety medication 80, 86

anticipatory grief 12–13, 33, 72, 113
antidepressant (medication) 80, 86, 113
anxiety 17–19, 27, 32, 33, 37, 42, 43, 47, 51, 57, 60, 61, 66, 71, 74, 83, 86, 93, 96, 98, 101–102, 104, 133, 137, 154; acute: 48; generalized anxiety disorder 18; reduction 108, 109, 111, 140
APA Monitor: Science Watch (journal) 144
apathy 11
Apercus: The Aphorisms of Mignon McLaughlin (McLaughlin, M.) 144
appetite changes 11, 42, 55, 57
appreciation 110, 123, 140, 151, 164, 168
Area Agency of Aging (AAA) 77
Aristotle 164
Armstrong Center for Music and Medicine 111
Asian Buddhism *see* Buddhism
atheism 21–22
Atlantic (magazine) 67
'aumakua see ancestral spirits
'Aumakua—Hawaiian Ancestral Spirits (Kane) 144
Austin Institute for the Study of Family and Culture 21
Australia 20, 117, 119, 143; Northern Territory 118
Australian Indigenous People 118–119
avoidance 49, 100, 116

balanced time perspective 2, 28, 31–32, 33, 34, 92, 99, 125, 129, 153
Balogi, L. 143
Barbara Karnes Publishing 147
bargaining 40, 41, 54, 66
Beck, J. 67
bedtime *see* sleep
belittling 83
benefits 98, 111, 124, 135, 139; finding 98, 104
Benson, Diane E. 120, 143
Berkeley, California 107
Berry, E.V. 144
Berry, J.W. 143
Beth Israel Medical Center 111

Index

betrayal 83
Bible study 127
Biddle, M. 104
biodegradable caskets 150
Blade Runner film 107
blame 27, 49, 83, 94, 95; deflecting 82; self 14, 83
Bles, Geoffrey 166
Block, S. 34
blood pressure: higher 78; lower 98, 104, 109, 112, 141
Bone, A. 145
Book Baby Publishing 144
boundaries 83, 86–87
Boyd, John 28, 35, 68, 145
brain 10, 47, 66–67, 99, 108, 111; electrochemical activity 71
bravery 167
breast cancer *see* cancer
breath/breathing technique 59–60, 63–66, 67, 110, 111, 115, 134, 135, 141
Brian 52–57, 94, 126–128
brighter future (time perspective) 3, 32, 58, 107, 115, 125, 126, 128–134, 139, 142, 152, 153
Brothers, Sisters, Strangers (Chapman) 82
Brunskill, Sarah 146
Buchinska, Daria (Dasha) x
Buddhism 21, 22, 93, 103, 112; Asian 22
Bueller, J.A. 105
burial 9, 20, 149; modern 149–150
burn out 129; caregiver 76

C. Nicki x
cancer 74, 80; breast 78; gastric 1, 39
caregiver/giving 72–80, 89, 102–103, 113; burnout 76
Carmody, J. 104
case workers 46
causal coherence *see* coherence
celebration of life 151
Center for Prolonged Grief (*prolonged grief. columbia.edu*) 171
Centers for Disease Control and Prevention 144
Central Council of the Tlingit and Haida Indian Tribes of Alaska *see* Tlingit
ceremonial pipe *see* smoking
Chapman, Fern Schumer 82, 104
character strengths 136–137, 167–169
charity *see* gifting charity
Charlot, John 121, 143
Cherry, Kendra 112, 143
chest pain 19, 54, 56
China 2, 42, 66, 163
Christianity 21, 44, 45, 120; Anglican 44; Church of England 45; Eastern Orthodox 45; Greek Orthodox (Church) 44; Non-Trinitarian 44; Protestant/Reformation 44, 124; Roman Catholic (Church) 44, 45, 46, 52
Christmas 80
chronic muscle tension *see* tension
Chung, C.K. 105
Church of England *see* Christianity
citizenship 168
civil rights 9
climate change 2, 8
clothing: black 45, 46; white 46
Coates, Hannah 134, 143
cognitive behavioral therapy 153, 154
coherence: causal 37; thematic 37
collective grief 7, 8, 13, 33
colonization 118
Colorado 111
Columbia University 171
common/normal grief 11, 13, 15, 33
communication 138
community 101
compassion 32, 92; self- 96–98, 104, 124, 165
complicated grief 13–14, 27, 33
compromise 165
concentrating, difficulty 11, 96
Confucius 163
confusion 83
Congleton, C. 104
connection 100–101, 104, 137, 139
consciousness 71
control 131, 131, 132, 140, 143; lack 115
cooperation 164
core beliefs 123
core values 72, 134, 137, 163–166, 167
cortisol 42
courage 167
Coutoumanos, Andria (Andie) x, 149
COVID-19 2, 8, 13, 35, 120, 171
covidgriefresources.com 171
CreativeSpirits.info 144
creativity 167
cremation 84, 119, 150
Cresswell, J.D. 105
cross-cultural 122
cross-generational 112
cryonics 149
cumulative grief 14–15, 33, 87
curiosity 167

Davidson, R.J. 57
decision making 107, 133, 141, 142
deep relaxation *see* relaxation
delayed gratification 91
delayed grief 14–15, 33
denial 40–41, 54, 66, 79, 80, 87
depersonalization 50
Depledge, M.H. 145
depression 8, 11, 15–17, 19, 27, 33, 37, 40, 41, 54, 60, 66, 71, 74, 77, 86, 93, 99–100, 103–

104, 107, 113, 116, 131, 133, 137, 154; major
16–17, 18, 44, 47; reduction 108, 111, 140, 141,
142, 143; situational 16, 41
derealization 50
detachment 14
diabetes 74
*Diagnostic and Statistical Manual (DSM)-5
Diagnostic Criterion for PTSD* 48–50
diet 132
Dinan, S. 34
Dipple, Michelle 1
disability 191
discernment 97, 136, 143
disenfranchised grief 15
diversity 165
Donnellan, M.B. 104
Drew, Chris 163, 166
drug abuse 74, 91, 96, 103
Dune 107
dysfunction 81

Eagleman, David 34, 68
East Coast *see* United States
Eastern European 122
Eastern Orthodox *see* Christianity
Edges (*edges.com.ua*) x
Egypt 29
electrochemical activity *see* brain
electrolytes 141
empathy 124, 138, 164, 165; lack 82
emptiness 11
England *see* United Kingdom
English 10
entitlement 81, 82, 83, 103
environment 99, 104, 108, 109, 118, 135, 141,
150
environmentalism 165
equality 164
estrangement 49, 86, 103
EternalReefs.com 150
Europe 2, 44, 123
European Center for the Environment &
Human Health 109
Everplans.com 68
expanded present (time perspective) 93, 96,
103, 153
expectations 37
experiential selfhood 118
expressive writing 98, 104

Facebook.com 151
FaceTime 117
fairness 164, 168
Family Friend Poems (*familyfriendpoems.
com*) 152
Far North *see* America
fear 9, 49, 55, 73, 131, 137
financial instability 9

First Nation 119
first responders 46, 48
five stages of grief 40–42
flashbacks 48, 54, 56, 57, 113, 114
Fleming, L.E. 145
flexibility 164
focus 13, 31–32, 43–44, 55, 58, 61–61, 63–65,
67, 71, 73, 76, 99, 101–102, 104, 115, 116, 117,
130, 134, 138, 142, 151; group 28; lack of 11,
14
Foley, Ben x
Food and Nutrition Board of the National
Research Council 141
Forbes (magazine) 144, 166
forgiveness 121–124, 165,168
Forneret, Alicia 171
Forty Day Party 120
Forum Media Polska (*FMP/e-forum.pl*) 2,
115
Four Loves (Lewis) 166
freedom *see* independence
freeze drying 149
friendship 164
frustration 74, 77, 89, 90
funeral 149
Funeral Friend (*thefuneralfriend.com*) 68
Funeral Guide (*funeralguide.co.uk*) 143
future (time perspective) 3, 4, 9, 28, 31, 32,
51, 56, 91, 96, 104, 107, 108, 114, 122, 124–125,
128–134, 136, 141, 142, 143, 153, 154; brighter
see brighter future (time perspective);
negative 125, 128, 130; positive 125, 127

Gabrenya, W.K. 143
Ganges River 84
Gans, K. 144, 145
Gard, J. 104
garden(ing) 101, 129, 138, 141
gaslighting 82
gastric cancer *see* cancer
generosity 107, 141, 165
gifting charity 151
glossary 153–154
goal(s) 76, 107, 111, 116, 141; setting 131–132,
142
God 84, 85, 92, 109, 164
Gone from My Sight: The Dying Experience
(Karnes) 147
Goodgrief.org 171
Goodtherapy.org 68
goodwill 164
Gould, W.R. 143
Grant, A.M. 143, 144
gratitude 109, 117, 123–124, 137, 140, 142, 143,
165, 168
Greater Good Magazine 107
Greater Good Science Center 107
greed 81, 103

Index

Greek Orthodox (Church) *see* Christianity
green burial 150
Grellier, J. 146
Grijalva, E. 104
Groundhog's Day (film) 41
guilt 11, 14, 41, 49, 50, 73, 76, 95, 98, 130, 139;
   -free 139; survivor's 94–95

hair shaving 118
Haleakala Crater 990
Haley, E. 34, 68
Halverson-Ramos, Faith 111, 144
*Handbook of Bereavement Research
   and Practice: Advances in Theory and
   Intervention* (Stroebe, Hansson, Schut) 35
*Handbook of Bereavement Research;
   Consequence, Coping and Care* (Stroebe,
   Hansson, Stroebe, Schut) 35
Hansenne, M. 144
Hansson, R.O. 35
Happify (*happify.com*) 1, 2, 28, 115, 171
happy/happiness/joy 3, 4, 11, 12, 31, 33, 43, 60,
   61, 66, 91, 95, 98, 99, 104, 109, 115, 116, 129,
   130–131, 133, 136–137, 138, 139, 140, 142, 143
Harms, P.D. 104
Harris, L. 166
Hartig, I. 146
Harvard Medical School 34
Hawai'i 75, 88, 120, 121
Hawaiian and Polynesian religion 121
headaches (migraine/tension) 63, 74, 103
Heady, B. 144
healing 38, 41, 62, 97, 108, 123, 129, 134
heart: 54. 110, 113; attack 75; disease 74;
   palpitations 19, 42; surgery 12
heaven 119
heirs 81
hell 119
Helpful Professor (*helpfulprofessor.com*)
   163, 166
helplessness 41, 83
Henrickson, H. 104
Heroic Imagination Project
   (*heroicimagination.org*) 2
Herrick, K. 144
high blood pressure *see* blood pressure
Himalayan singing bowls *see* singing bowls
Hina 113
Hinduism 21, 83–84
History.com 104
Holmes and Rahe Stress Scale 19, 34
Holter, Sarah x
Holzel, B.K. 104
honesty 165
ho'oponopono 122–124, 142
hope 115, 116, 117, 134, 168
hospice 77, 78–79, 103
Hospice Foundation of America 171

housekeeping 76
Hudson, J.A. 144
hugs 117, 124, 137
humanity 168
humility 165, 168
humor 168
The Hunger Games book (Collins)/film 107
hydration *see* water
hypertension *see* blood pressure
hypervigilance 49

Idemoudia, E.S. 143
ignoring 83
imagination 128, 120
imua 122
in-home respite 77
Incognito: The Secret Lives of the Brain
   (Eagleman) 34
independence 73, 127
India 84, 93
Indigenous: cultures 21, 22, 93, 103, 143;
   people 20, 117, 122, 143
Indus Valley 83
infighting 81
insomnia 61, 96
Institute of Medicine 141, 144
Institute of Medicine of the National
   Archives 141, 144
integrity 167
intensified feelings 11
Interstellar (film) 107
intrapersonal 124
invalidating 83
irritability *see* anger
Islam 21, 84–85
isolation 11, 14, 16, 41, 77, 95, 100, 101, 104
Italy 78; Capri 78

Jackson, L.T.B. 143
jealousy 83
Jefferson, North Carolina 35, 105, 145
The Jetsons (cartoon) 107
Journal of Experimental Child Psychology
   144
Journal of Loss and Trauma 34
*Journal of Loss and Trauma: International
   Perspectives on Stress and Coping* 145
Journal of Positive Psychology 144, 145
joy *see* happiness
Juan, S. 34, 68
Judaism 21, 84–85, 124
justice 168

Kaddish (Mourner's) 85
Kalidasa 93
Kamidana-fuji 22
Kane, H.K. 144
Karnes, Barbara 147

Karta 84
Kashdan, T.B. 145
Kessler, David 40
Khandobina, Natalia x
Kilpatrick, L.A. 105
kind(ness) 96, 107–108, 116, 124, 137, 140, 141, 142, 165, 168; random acts 102, 116, 142
Klemenko, E. 143
knowledge 167
Korff, J. 144
Kravitz, Len 140, 144
Krippner, Stanley (Stan) x
Krull, E. 68
Kubler-Ross, Elizabeth 38, 40, 41, 66, 68

lack of concentration 47, 49, 57, 115
lack of empathy *see* empathy
Lanham, Maryland 34
Last Will and Testament/Living Will 81, 87–88, 103
Lazar, S.W. 104
leadership, 168
Learned Optimism: How to Change Your Mind and Your Life (Seligman, M,E,) 144
Lee, B. 105
Lewis, C.S. 166
Lexington Books 34
life force *see* mana
Life Magazine 40
Lily 55, 57, 94
LiveScience.com 149
Living and Loving Better: Healing from the Past, Embracing the Present, Creating an Ideal Future (Zimbardo and Sword) 1, 105, 114, 145
living dead *see* ancestors
Living Will *see* Last Will and Testament
London, UK 35, 145, 166, 169
loneliness 10, 11, 33
Loren, Sophia 78
Lorenz, L. 34
Loss and Anticipatory Grief (Rando) 34
loss of a baby 171
love 10, 73, 89, 117, 120, 121, 124, 133, 136, 137, 140, 142, 13, 163, 168; agape 164; of learning 167; romantic 164; unconditional 164
low blood pressure *see* blood pressure
Lowey, Joanne 111
loyalty 166
lying 82
Lyuborminsky, Sonja 140, 144

Maciejewski, P.K. 34
Maitoza, R. 34
major depression *see* depression
Makobe-Rabothata, M. 143
mana: life force 138; sacred energy 121; spiritual quality 121

manipulation 83
March of Dimes 171
Marcilino, Ueslei 120, 144
Mark, J. 34
mass shootings/murders (United States) 2, 8
Massachusetts 110
Massimino, John 78
Massimino, Neva 78
Masters, Robert 172
material realm 118
Mayer, E.A. 105
Mayo Clinic 34, 86, 105
McFarland & Company, Inc., Publishers 114, 145
McLaughlin, M. 144
McKewen, B.S. 67
meal delivery 76
meaningful life 4, 31, 33, 98, 136, 137, 138, 139, 142, 143
Mecca 84
Medicare 79
medicine man 119
meditation 84, 93, 103, 134, 151
Meiring, D. 143
Memorial Day 121
memorial service 9
Mendoza, Marilyn 23, 34
mercy 168
Midwest *see* United States
migraine *see* headache
Mikolajczak, M. 144
military method of sleep *see* sleep
mindfulness 93, 99, 171
mini-break 116, 142
ministroke *see* stroke
miscarriage 8, 171
moderation 168
modern burial *see* burial
modesty 168
Monoahan, M. 143
Moore, M. 34
Moralis, S. 34
morphic resonance 21
mortality 74
Mourner's Kaddish *see* Kaddish
mourning 8–9, 20, 21, 22–27, 33, 42, 44, 45, 46, 66, 83–85, 98, 100–101, 108, 112–115, 117–121, 125, 130, 137, 139, 142
Muhammed 84
mummification 149
murders *see* mass shootings
music 110–111, 141; therapy 111
musical anhedonia 111
Muslim 84

Naliboff, B.D. 105
naming protocols 118
napping *see* sleep

Index

narcissism/Narcissistic Personality Disorder 81–83, 85–87, 103
narrative 37, 38, 42, 43, 66
Nash, J. 169
National Cancer Institute 34
National Geographic 35
National Institute of Health 68, 105
National Institute of Mental Health (NIMH) 16, 17, 19, 34
National Institute on Aging 105
National Library of Medicine 68
National Research Council 141
National Suicide and Crisis Lifeline (9-8-8) 17
Native American 122
Native Hawaiian 121,122
natural burial *see* green burial
nature 108–110, 119, 131, 133, 136–137, 141
Nature Neuroscience (journal) 67
Navajo 119
Neanderthal 20
Neff Hernandez, Michele 1
NeuroImage (journal) 104
Neuroscience News (magazine) 144
New Age spirituality 21
New Social Worker (magazine) 34
New York 105, 112, 144; Bronx 78; City 43
New Yorker (magazine) 68
New Zealand 120
Newman, D.A. 104
Newsweek (magazine) 105
Nineteen-Eighty-Four (*1984*, Orwell) 107
Nobel Prize (Physics) 71
Noelle 52–58, 94–95, 126–128
Non-Trinitarian *see* Christianity
nonbelievers/nones 21
normal grief *see* common grief
North American 119
Northern Territory *see* Australia
Northwestern University 144
nursing home 77, 79, 80

O'Bryan, Amanda 172
obsessive-compulsive 56
Oishi, S. 145
On Death and Dying (Ross) 40, 66, 68
On Grief and Grieving (Ross and Kessler) 40
open-mindedness 166, 167
optimistic 98, 104, 107, 133, 142, 166, 268
Organizational Behavior and Human Decision Processes, III (Grant and Sonnentag) 144
O'Rourke, M. 68
overwhelm 103, 113
Oxford, United Kingdom 105
Oxford English Dictionary 82, 105, 169
Oxford Handbook of Health Psychology (Pennebaker and Chung) 105
Oxford University Press 105

Pacific Islands 120, 121
paddle-out ceremony 151
pain 18, 41, 73, 74, 78, 79, 81, 88, 101, 103, 113, 129; reduction 141; relief 112
Pakistan 83
palpitations *see* heart
panic attack/disorder 18, 54, 56
Papa, A. 34
Pappas, Stephanie 149
parasympathetic nerve system 135
Passover 85
past negative (time perspective) 2, 3, 28, 31, 32, 43, 44, 47, 51, 56–58, 61, 66, 67, 90, 96, 114, 125, 130, 153 154
past positive (time perspective) 3, 28, 31, 43, 44, 51, 56–61, 66, 67, 91, 95, 96, 104, 114, 129, 140, 142, 153, 154
Pathway Centers for Grief and Loss 171
patience 166
paying it forward 137
Pennebaker, J.W. 105
Perry, C. 144
perseverance 166
persistence 167
personal identity 9
personal values *see* core values
Personality and Individual Differences (journal) 144
Peterson, C. 105
pets 101, 109, 110, 135
Pew Research Center 21
Planck, Max 71
Planet Earth 109
plastination 149
Poland 2, 115, 123
police officers 48
Polynesia 20, 117, 120–121, 123, 120–121, 143; theology 121
Portland, Oregon 144
positive psychology 167
PositivePsychology.com 169
post-loss grief 13
post-mortem photography 45
post-traumatic stress disorder (PTSD) 1, 2, 10, 33, 44, 46, 50, 54, 56, 57, 66, 74, 80, 92, 94, 96, 97, 100, 101, 104, 107, 113, 115, 125, 154
Pott, Leanne 149
pounding heart *see* heart; palpitations
Praghakar, J. 144
Preta-Karma 84
present fatalistic (time perspective) 3, 28, 31, 32, 56, 71, 90, 94–97, 99, 101–104, 113, 125, 129, 130, 131, 142, 153, 154; temporary 103, 153
present hedonistic (time perspective) 3, 28, 31, 32, 56, 71, 90–91, 93–96, 99–103; selected 3, 71, 91, 92, 95, 96, 114, 139 153, 154
Prigerson, H. 34

primary care physician (PCP) 79, 112
Primer in Positive Psychology (Peterson) 105
Prince Albert 45
probate 81
Probst, J. 144
prolonged grief 14, 15
prosocial 100–102
prospection 107
Protestant Reformation *see* Christianity
Protestantism *see* Christianity
prudence 168
Psychcentral.com 34
Psychiatry Research 104
Psychological Bulletin (journal) 104
Psychology in Practice 115
Psychologytoday.com 34, 88, 104, 105, 115, 145, 166, 172
psychotic (situational) 55, 57

quality of life 78, 103, 111
quantum field 21
quantum theory 71
Queen Victoria 45
questioning 11
Quoidbach, J. 144
Qur'an 84

racing heart *see* heart; palpitations
Rando, T.A. 34
random acts of kindness *see* kind(ness)
Recovery Village (*ridgefieldrecovery.com*) 68
reflection 62, 121; deep 142
Register (*theregister.com*) 34, 68
regret 9, 121, 129
reincarnation 84, 118, 119
rejuvenation 62, 110
relationships 11, 12, 32, 72, 73, 80, 97, 100, 101, 104, 137, 140, 143, 163; parent-child 81–83, 85–87, 96; siblings 82–83; toxic 76, 82, 86
Relax and Win: Championship Performance (Winter, Lloyd Bud) 134–135
relaxation 112; deep 62–67, 134–136
religious beliefs/practices *see* spiritual beliefs/practices
remembrance 151, 152
remorse 123
resentment 81
resilience 98
resomation 149
respect 166
respite care 79
Reuters.com 120, 144
Rider Publishing 35
rivalry 83
River of Time video (https://www.youtube.com/ watch?v=r4ZX0XVAa2A&t=256s) 56, 172
Robins, R.W. 104

Roman Catholic (Church) *see* Christianity
romantic love *see* love
Rossinger, A. 144
Roy, K. 34
Royal College of Psychiatrists Publishing 169
Russia 10, 115

Sabina, Laura 152
sacred energy *see mana*
sad(ness) 10, 14, 47, 55, 74, 75, 78, 79, 95, 96, 101, 103, 112, 115, 130
St. Martin's Press Publishing 105
Salat al Janazah 84
Samoa 120
Samuelson, Marnie Crawford 110, 145
San Francisco, California 105, 145
Sanskrit 93
Saudi Arabia 84
Saybrook University x
Schut, H. 35
ScienceDaily.com 104
Scientific American (magazine) 21, 104
Scientific Reports (journal) 145
Scribner Publishing 68
Seaburn, David 71, 105
Sealaska Heritage Institute 144
SealaskaHeritage.org 120
selected present hedonistic *see* present hedonistic
self-awareness 142
self-blame *see* blame
self-compassion *see* compassion
self-confidence *see* self-esteem
self-discipline 166
self-doubt 83
self-esteem 109, 125, 131, 137, 139, 140, 142
self-harm 27
self-hypnosis 135
self-medication 14
self-reflection 97
self-regulation 168
self-talk 97
Seligman, M.E. 144
setting goals *see* goals
sex (intimacy) 88–90, 91
shape-shifting 83
Shared Grief Project (*sharedgrief.org*) 171
Shavuot 85
Shear, K. 68
Sheldon, K.M. 144
Sheloshim 85
Shemini Atzeret 85
Sherman, Michael 21
shiva 85
shock 40, 81
short-term nursing home *see* nursing home
singing bowls: Himalayan/Tibetan 112, 141

Index

situational depression *see* depression
situationally psychotic *see* psychotic
Skype 151
sleep/bedtime 11, 18, 47, 49, 54, 59, 61–66, 67, 74, 77, 116, 134–136, 143; deprivation/disturbance 96, 113; improve 112; military method 134–136; napping 136
Smith, S.R. 105
smoking 78; special ceremonial pipe 119
smudging 119
Soaring Spirits International (*soaringspirits. org*) 1, 171
Social Indicators Research (journal) 144
social intelligence 168
social justice 166
Sorry Business 118
sound baths 112
sound therapy 112, 141
Soundwell Music Therapy (*soundwellmusictherapy.com*) 144
South America 120
space burial 149
special ceremonial pipe *see* smoking
Spence, G.B. 144
Spencer, M. 169
spirit ancestors *see* ancestral spirits
spirit world 118
spiritual beliefs/practices 11, 20–22, 29, 83, 92, 93, 103, 109, 110, 117–121, 122, 163
spiritual leader 119
spiritual quality *see mana*
spiritual selfhood 118
spirituality 128, 168
Spirituality and Health (magazine) 145
sports 130, 139
Springer Publishing 145
sraddha 84
Star Trek (films /television shows) 107
Steger, M.F. 145
stomach ache/problems 15, 18
Stosney, Steven 163, 166
stress 18–20, 33, 42, 54, 57, 62–63, 67, 73–74, 81, 86, 102, 103, 113, 116, 151; reduction 108, 111, 112, 140, 141, 143
Stroebe, H. 35
Stroebe, M.S. 35
stroke/transient ischemic attack 75
subconscious 55, 113
suicide 15, 17, 55, 57
Suicide and Crisis Hotline (9-8-8) 172
support (system) 12, 74–75, 76, 78, 79, 103
survivor's guilt *see* guilt
Suyenobu, B.Y. 105
Switzerland 38
Sword, Richard M. (Rick) x, 1, 39, 68, 74–75, 79–80, 88–90, 112–114, 122, 145, 146, 154, 172
Sword, Rosemary KM (Rose) 35, 39, 68,

74–75, 79–80, 88–90, 105, 112–115, 122, 145, 146, 154, 171, 172
Synergy Wellness (*sysnergywellnesscenter. com*) 105

Tahiti 120
Taliban 95
Tay, L. 104
Taylor-Desir, M. 68
temperance 168
temporary present fatalistic *see* present fatalistic
tension (chronic muscle) 63
tension headache *see* headache
Tereschenko, Olha, x
terminally ill/terminal illness 38, 41, 66, 72, 78, 96, 103
Than, K. 35
thematic coherence *see* coherence
thoughtfulness 166
Tibetan singing bowls *see* singing bowls
Tillisch, K. 105
Time Cure: Overcoming PTSD with the New Psychology of Time Perspective Therapy (Zimbardo, Sword and Sword) 1, 88, 105, 114
Time Paradox: The new psychology of time that will change your life (Zimbardo and Boyd) 35
Time Paradox.com 172
time perspective therapy (TPT) x, 1, 2, 3, 29, 42, 46, 52, 54, 56, 57, 60, 91, 94–96, 111–114, 122, 126–128, 154, 172
time perspectives 2, 28, 51, 153, 154
Tlingit 120; Central Council of the Tlingit and Haida Indian Tribes of Alaska 120, 143, 145
tolerance 166
Tonga 120
toxic relationships *see* relationships
transcendence 168
Transcendental-future Time Perspective Inventory 28, 29, 154
transient ischemic attack *see* stroke
transportation 76
trauma *see* post-traumatic stress disorder (PTSD)
triangulating 83
Trust & Will (*trustandwill.com*) 152
Tulane Medical School Department of Psychiatry 23
Twin Peaks Creative 172

Ukraine x, 2, 115
Unbridled and Extreme Present Hedonism in B. Lee (Ed) *Dangerous Case of Donald Trump: 27 Psychiatrists and Mental Health Experts Assess a President* (Zimbardo, P. and Sword, R.) 105

Index

unconditional love see love
underworld 120
United Kingdom/England 45
United Nations 117, 145, 171
United States of America 2, 38, 51, 75,
    78, 113, 122, 171, 172; East Coast 80, 113;
    Midwest 88
University of Coimbra, Portugal 146
University of Colorado School of Medicine 38
University of Exeter 109
University of Hawaii 121
University of New Mexico 140
unkind 23

vaccinations 77
Values Institute (values.institute) 166
Vancouver, Washington 147
Van de Vijver, F.J.R. 143
Van Dyke, Henry 5, 36, 69, 106, 147
Vangel, M. 104
Ventura, Dee Ann x
Ventura, Scott x
VeryWellMind.com 112
Victoria Public Sector Commission 145
Victorian Era 45
Vintage Books Publishing 144
virtues see core values
visual arts 110
visualization 132
vitality 167
volunteering 139

war veterans 94, 95
Warber, S.I. 145
warm moments 137–138
Warsaw, Poland 122
Washington, DC 35
water (importance of; hydration) 77,
    140–141, 143
Weir, K. 35
Western culture/societies 38, 45, 93, 112, 122
What Is Spirituality: A Personal Exploration
    (Spencer, M.) 169
WhatsYourGrief.com 171
Wheeler, B.W. 146
White, Matthew P. 109, 146

WhyGriefMatters.org 171
WiderImage/Reuters.com 144
widowed (men/women) 9, 10, 17, 18
Wiley Publishing 105, 145
will see Last Will and Testament
Williams, L. 34, 68
Willis, Claire B. 110, 146
Wilson, Christina 1172
Winter, Lloyd Bud 134–135
wisdom 167
withdrawal see isolation
Wong, C. 145
workaholic 31, 129, 142
World Data: The World in Numbers
    (worlddata.info) 68
World Health Organization 171
World Psychiatry (journal) 68

Xia Dynasty 163
Xingu 120

yahrzeit 85
Yan, T. 104
Yannell, Ian x
Yannell, Liz x
Yannell, Michael x
Yerramsetti, S.M. 104
yizkor 85
Yom Kippur 85
YouTube.com 172

Zhang, B. 34
Zimbardo, Don 78
Zimbardo, George 78
Zimbardo, Margaret 78
Zimbardo, Philip G. (Phil) 28, 35, 68, 78, 88,
    105, 114, 115, 145, 146, 154, 171, 172
Zimbardo, Vera 78
Zimbardo temporal theory 154
Zimbardo Time Perspective Inventory
    (ZTPI) 28–29, 56, 58, 66, 71, 91, 96; graph
    162; long form 155–161; short form 29–30,
    154, 172
Zisook, S. 68
Zoom 62, 117, 151